INVESTOR ORIENTED CORPORATE SOCIAL RESPONSIBILITY REPORTING

Reporting organizations' corporate social responsibility activities is difficult – a lack of regulation means that the communication of these activities varies significantly and there is a multitude of ways in which mistakes can be made.

The author provides the tools and insights required to produce investor-friendly CSR reports, and includes a chapter showing how investors can integrate CSR in their quantified analysis of investment opportunities. Features include formulas, conversion standards, and CSR note tables, which enable the book to be used as a practical handbook as well as in the classroom.

Written by an experienced compliance officer with years of experience in reporting CSR, this book is an easy-to-follow guide for practitioners and students and will be required reading for students of accounting, financial reporting, and auditing as well as those in industry who want to improve their organization's reporting standards.

Jane Thostrup Jagd is Director and Control Compliance Officer at A.P. Moller-Maersk A/S, Denmark.

This book provides a practical toolkit to students, analysts and investors on CSR reporting in the current integrated reporting environment where the linkage between financial and non-financial is absolutely critical.

Sumit Lodhia, *Professor, University of South Australia, Australia*

Responsible investment increasingly relies on CSR reporting to generate sustainable value. While the demand for CSR information is widespread, a challenge for financial analysts remains to distil the right information before making an appropriate investment decision. Based on a large set of examples of CSR reporting, this book provides practical insights on how to successfully integrate CSR into mainstream financial decisions.

Paolo Perego, *Associate Professor in Management Accounting, Erasmus University Rotterdam, Netherlands*

Dr Jagd is to be congratulated for conducting this investigation into CSR reporting among the largest corporations in the world. For both investors and policy makers this exercise lifts the lid on the significant uncertainties surrounding the newly emerging and rapidly growing sphere of corporate social responsibility. As we move towards the 10 billion people planet and then the inexorable reduction that will follow, providing reporters and their stakeholders with a simple tool kit for effective CSR reporting will become an invaluable asset.

Dr Steve Priddy, *Director of Research, London School of Business and Finance, UK*

INVESTOR ORIENTED CORPORATE SOCIAL RESPONSIBILITY REPORTING

Jane Thostrup Jagd

Routledge
Taylor & Francis Group

LONDON AND NEW YORK

First published 2015
by Routledge
2 Park Square, Milton Park, Abingdon, Oxon OX11 1D.N

and by Routledge
711 Third Avenue, New York, NY 10017

Routledge is an imprint of the Taylor & Francis Group, an informa business

British Library Cataloguing in Publication Data
A catalogue record for this book is available from the British Library

Library of Congress Cataloging in Publication Data
Jagd, Jane Thostrup.
Investor oriented corporate social responsibility reporting / Jane Thostrup Jagd. – First Edition.
   pages cm
   1. Social responsibility of business. 2. Social accounting. I. Title.
   HD60.J34 2014
   658.4'08–dc23
   2014002134

ISBN: 978-1-138-01583-8 (hbk)
ISBN: 978-1-138-01584-5 (pbk)
ISBN: 978-1-315-79411-2 (ebk)

Typeset in Bembo
by Sunrise Setting Ltd, Paignton, UK

CONTENTS

List of figures *vii*
List of tables *viii*
Foreword *ix*

1 **Why is there a need for this book?** **1**

2 **Is CSR profitable?** **4**

 Criticism of CSR rating agencies 7
 Conclusion 10

3 **Rules and guidelines that exist** **12**

 OECD Guidelines for Multinational Enterprises 14
 United Nations Global Compact (UNGC) 14
 ISO 26000 16
 Greenhouse Gas (GHG) Protocol Initiative 17
 Global Reporting Initiative (GRI) 18
 AA1000 series – especially AA1000AS 22
 ISAE 3000 23
 International Integrated Reporting Council (IIRC) 27
 Principles for Responsible Investments (PRI) 29
 How much are the guidelines used? 31

4 **Rules that ought to exist** **33**

 How can we ensure that CSR reports
  are useful to investors? 34
 Financial vs operational boundaries 36

Financial consolidation method 41
Standard form for a minimum of CSR reporting 42
Integrated reporting 43
CSR accounting principles 49

5 Proposed minimum data   **53**

Environmental data 60
Social data 67
Governance data 75

6 Evidence requirements for valid and complete data   **78**

Requirements for documentation 78
Data types 79

7 How to create a good control environment   **82**

Local work organization within a control environment 84
Headquarter tasks to ensure the control environment 95

**8 How can investors use CSR in their
analysis of stocks?**   **100**

Triple Bottom Line 101
Combined KPIs 105

9 Conclusion   **111**

Appendices

A Definition of CSR and other abbreviations 113
B People interviewed for this book 116
C Company overview 117
D XBRL 121
*E Conversion standards for energy, volume, weight,
  and mass 123*
F Formulas 125
G CSR note forms 129

References   *136*
Index   *142*

Figures

3.1 Signs of weak evidence   24
4.1 WestLB's appropriate question to Cadbury
Schweppes' CSR Report 2006   44
7.1 Annual process to ensure the control environment   84
7.2 Risk diagram   88
7.3 Maturity decision tree for controls   89
7.4 Overview of the control environment
per control objective   91
8.1 Cash outflow distribution   101
8.2 P/E versus P/CSR – the investor logical tool   107
8.3 P/E versus P/CO_2e for utility companies
on CDP's Global 500 reports   108
C.1 Geographical split of 50 largest listed
companies' headquarters   117

Tables

3.1	Historical development of CSR initiatives, regulations, and guidelines	12
3.2	UNGC's ten principles	16
5.1	Differences in OECD FTE reporting methodologies	68
5.2	When is an employee a leader?	70
7.1	Risk assessment of wrong reporting	86
8.1	PUMA's euro standards for environmental impact, 2010	104
C.1	The 50 largest listed companies 2012, according to Forbes Fortune 2000	118
E.1	Energy conversion standards	123
E.2	Volume conversion standards	124
E.3	Weight and mass conversion standards	124
G.1	Classic CSR note	129
G.2	Integrated note	132

FOREWORD

This book is intended to be a textbook for student auditors so that they can provide guidance on and review the corporate social responsibility (CSR) reporting by companies, but it is also designed to be a textbook for financial students and financial investors, guiding them as to why they should, and in how they can, use CSR reports in their analysis of the stock markets.

But the book will also help companies who wish to develop more investor-friendly CSR reporting, or those who are required to report on CSR for the first time and want a good start. The book provides, inter alia, answers to fundamental questions such as:

- How can the company's CSR figures be added up, so it is not apples and oranges mixed together, and so the figures are in a context in which they make sense? Context-free figures make no sense.
- How is it that a subsidiary in Uganda or China can report valid data on water consumption, although they have no invoices?
- How does the company measure CO_2 emissions and secure supporting evidence?
- How does the company measure the size of its workforce and why is that important?
- How can it be ensured that each company's emissions are comparable to other companies' emissions, so that the comparisons are meaningful and useful for investors?

The book also provides instructions on how a company can establish a good control environment for its CSR reporting, which is equivalent to its financial control environment. Hence, the book helps to show how CSR reporting can emerge from its position as the annual report's stepchild, which some investors have difficulties in taking seriously.

The book's appendices include conversion tables, formulas, and reporting schedules for minimum data, which, combined with the chapter on proposals for minimum data, can serve as an important reference tool for companies and investors.

The book is a self-contained independent research project that has been conducted through interviews with various key individuals of international standing, through an analysis of the 50 largest listed companies' CSR reports, through an extensive literature review,[1] and, not least, as an outcome of several years of practical experience in collecting, validating, and consolidating the CSR data of A. P. Moller-Maersk's more than 1,000 legal entities' CSR reporting into the annual group reports. The book is not an expression of A. P. Moller-Maersk's attitudes.

The author would like to thank all interviewees for participating and the Carbon Disclosure Project (CDP) for providing a large CO_2 data set, which is used to illustrate how investors can include non-financial data in their analysis.

Happy reading!

Note

1   Jagd (2013).

1

WHY IS THERE A NEED FOR THIS BOOK?

Today in many countries such as South Africa, Denmark, and France the vast majority of the largest companies produce some form of corporate social responsibility (CSR) reporting – not least because it is mandated by their countries' financial statements acts. However, when asked about the importance of this reporting, many companies, auditors, and investors contend that it is of limited value. Alan Teixeira, Senior Director, International Accounting Standards Board (IASB), puts it this way: "Some businesses take it very seriously, some use it more opportunistically (i.e. as a PR/marketing exercise) and some ignore it. My sense is that where elements of CSR are in regulation businesses treat it mainly as a compliance exercise."[1] Some indicate it primarily affects companies internally. "The CSR reporting, established today, is usually mostly important for the company itself. It is a kind of status whereby the company's own employees and management can see an overall picture of the CSR activities undertaken during the year and what goals are met or the evolution herein."[2]

Financially and non-financially, if CSR reporting is to be useful to others, it should be possible to compare content across companies and over time. The data must be validated and must be easily accessible; this will provide the foundations for investors to be able to use the reporting in their analysis of corporate risks and performance. Whereas there are many specific international and national rules on financial reporting, unfortunately the regulations on CSR reporting are not very specific. "Consistency is very important to investors, so the use of international standards for sustainability reporting is a key factor when looking to get investors to incorporate the topic into their analysis."[3] Thus, one of the cornerstones of useful CSR reporting is not yet in place.

The lack of precision in the regulations means that we have thousands of annual reports of very variable quality. Thus, we are also in the position that thousands of companies use resources to develop CSR reporting, which from an overall perspective can effectively be used for very little. Companies report on different aspects, they measure them differently, and it is often the case that a company cannot even compare its own CO_2 data with, for example, its production data as the boundaries and consolidation of CSR data are different from financial consolidation. Thus, one cannot really comment on whether the company is performing well or poorly, environmentally, either in itself as a company or in relation to other companies.

However, recent research[4] shows that valid CSR reporting places the professional investor in a far better position to value the company properly and it creates fewer fluctuations in stock prices when negative events occur. Similarly, it also appears that valid CSR reporting can actually reduce capital costs. Therefore, "…it is clear that increased transparency creates trust, and provides a more holistic picture and there are more confident long-term investors."[5]

The above arguments mean that if investors are to acquire the described benefits, it is at least necessary that the CSR reports can be used by investors when they evaluate companies; it also requires that CSR reports are available, comparable, and validated. According to a recent survey undertaken by the Association of Chartered Certified Accountants (ACCA) and the European Sustainable Investment Forum (Eurosif), a number of issues are explicitly mentioned by investors when asked about the usability of the current CSR reporting:[6]

- Current non-financial reporting by companies is inadequate for investors.
- Reporting must be linked to business risk and integrated with financial information.
- Quantitative key performance indicators (KPIs) are essential.
- Accountability and assurance mechanisms are needed.

Addressing the above points requires data discipline. For companies who want a stable share price or capital, a valid CSR report in a familiar format suitable for investors is an important tool both for the company and the investor.

The book is structured such that it begins with a chapter presenting arguments on whether CSR is worthwhile and the uses to which investors can actually put CSR reporting. The rules and guidelines that currently exist internationally are presented, followed by a section on the rules that ought to exist if investors are to maximize the benefits of CSR reporting. Through an analysis of the 50 largest listed companies' CSR reports, in conjunction with an analysis of what equity research agencies seek from CSR information, a set of minimum data that all companies can use is then proposed; these minimum data will be defined quite specifically including demands for evidence. It is also demonstrated that companies must ensure that the data are valid and complete through a structured control environment, whereby reviewers can assure accountability.

The book concludes with a chapter that shows how to combine these available, comparable, and validated CSR data with financial data, so that CSR data are immediately usable by the investor.

Appendix A contains definitions of abbreviations, and Appendix B lists those interviewed for this book. In addition, for reference purposes, other appendices contain formulas, conversion tables, and reporting forms.

Notes

1   Interview with Alan Teixeira, Senior Director, IASB.
2   Interview with State Authorized Auditor Birgitte Mogensen, former PWC Partner, CSR – now owner of Board Management.
3   Interview with Gordon Hewitt, Sustainability Advisor, Association of Chartered Certified Accountants (ACCA).
4   Dhaliwal *et al.* (2011); Flammer (2012).
5   Interview with Dr Nancy Kamp-Roelands, former Executive Director, Ernst & Young, Corporate Responsibility, the Netherlands and Belgium – now Deputy Director of the International Auditing and Assurance Standards Board (IAASB).
6   ACCA & Eurosif (2013).

2
IS CSR PROFITABLE?

Since CSR was launched as an idea in the 1970s, countless attempts have been made to answer the question of its profitability. Why should the company as a profit-generating unit deal with CSR at all – is it not pure philanthropy? Very different answers to this question exist.

One of the most-cited meta-analyses[1] is from 2003 and covers the period 1972–1997; through a review of 52 academic studies it concludes that there is a positive correlation between CSR and financial performance. Conversely, a British analysis[2] of 451 FTSE All Share Index companies as of 1 July 2002 finds that the least socially responsible companies achieved by far the best profitability. This analysis also shows that the otherwise prevailing explanation for this phenomenon, the so-called sector beta – i.e. the volatility associated with various sectors, of which some are more likely, or have a longer history, than others to carry out CSR reporting – can only partly explain this underperformance.

A recent meta-analysis[3] of 251 pieces of research, covering the period 1972–2007, shows the opposite – that there is a very small, but only a very small, positive correlation between CSR and financial performance.

Thus, we cannot give an unambiguous scientific answer to the fundamental question "Is CSR profitable?" But why should it be particularly profitable to be a CSR-oriented company?

There are at least five arguments for this:[4]

- Customers will prefer products/services from CSR-oriented companies.
- Investors will prefer responsible companies, whereby the company capital costs will decrease.
- Talented employees will increasingly be attracted to employment in a responsible company.

- Responsible companies will be more innovative.
- Companies that enjoy a high level of public trust will be less exposed to risks from safety, boycotts, or other loss of reputation.

Many of these arguments are not especially easy to verify or reject scientifically, although various attempts have been made.[5] In particular, the argument concerning capital costs has been examined many times, with different conclusions. An extensive analysis[6] of the first-time CSR reports of American companies and their potential impact on the cost of capital shows that the cost of capital decreases during the year in which the company publishes its first CSR report compared with the cost of capital in the preceding year. Furthermore, it can be shown that companies that have a better CSR rating (KLD[7]) than their competitors continue to have lower capital costs than their competitors in the years after the publication of their first CSR report.

Finally, analysis shows that these highly CSR-rated companies attract more institutional investors than their competitors, and that these investors make fewer forecast errors than they do for the investments they have made in companies without this high CSR rating; moreover, these institutional investors are willing to invest significantly higher amounts than otherwise in those companies that undertake CSR reporting. This conclusion, drawn about institutional investors' much stronger interest in, and response to, CSR reporting compared with individual investors, is also demonstrated in a Chinese analysis,[8] which was undertaken following the 2008 Chinese milk scandal.[9]

However, another large British analysis[10] of 20,715 observations for the period 1993–2008 shows, for example, that these capital-cost analyses also depend on the time from which the data stem. Equity analysts' buy/hold/sell recommendations are compared with companies' CSR rating in KLD over time, and it is shown that strong CSR ratings up until 1997 actually have a negative effect on equity analysts' recommendations. After 1999, the opposite is apparent – one can see a positive correlation between high CSR ratings and equity analysts' recommendations. One cannot, however, show the opposite – that weak CSR ratings generally result in negative investment recommendations.

In the same study it is also shown that those companies with high visibility (measured by their market value) receive both strongly positive and negative responses from the market, from a strong or weak CSR rating, respectively. Finally, the analysis also indicates that the so-called advanced analysts (e.g. JP Morgan and Deutsche Bank), which the researchers have noted as more CSR-oriented, have a tendency to provide a higher buying recommendation for firms with a high CSR rating, while they do not "punish" those companies that have a weaker CSR rating. It is therefore concluded that not only is it to the advantage of all companies to have a CSR rating, whether good or bad, as it can create lower capital costs for the company, but also larger companies with significant media attention must be very conscious of ensuring a good CSR rating, as this is reflected directly in their share prices.

A modification to the aforementioned result can be seen in a large American event analysis,[11] which demonstrates that the negative impact of detrimental environmental events on share prices has increased in recent years, while the impact of positive environmental business initiatives on share prices has decreased. The analysis also shows that if a company generally has a good CSR rating in the KLD, then this has an insuring effect, as the negative impact on share prices from environmental events is diminished. Additionally, the analysis shows that a good CSR rating actually has a further dampening effect on share prices when the company undertakes additional environmental initiatives. This means that at any given time when a company has achieved a good CSR rating, there is then no or only a very marginal effect from taking further environmental initiatives. Therefore, an optimal point is likely to exist at which further environmental initiatives do not benefit the investor. There is also research[12] showing that companies in which the management has no significant shareholding have a tendency to overinvest in CSR; it is believed this is intended only to benefit the managers' own reputation as good corporate citizens. There is therefore a limit to how much CSR is of benefit to companies and investors.

The above is in line with the analysis by Margolis *et al.* (2009), which also shows that "doing bad, if discovered, has a more pronounced effect on financial performance than doing good" (p. 23), so maybe the relationship is less straightforward: perhaps it is not whether CSR is profitable, but rather that a lack of CSR does not pay.

However, the analysis referenced above also shows that when some investors expressed to ACCA in 2008 about CSR reporting that "…speaking purely from an investment analyst perspective, it's not useful at all…" or "…absolutely useless from my point of view", it was probably disingenuous.[13] CSR reporting has a proven connection to share prices, and in particular it has an influence as a form of "insurance" in relation to companies' reputations during particularly negative events – perhaps especially for institutional investors.

Criticism of CSR rating agencies

As described initially, it is not yet possible to draw firm conclusions on whether there is a direct negative or positive relationship between CSR and corporate profitability. This is probably not least due to the fact that the currently available CSR data are not particularly valid for analytical purposes. Since in many countries it is not currently required by law that all companies must publish a CSR report to a certain standard, with a particular set of indicators calculated using an exact framework, one can really only measure the CSR performance of those companies that choose to publish a CSR report – and it is typically only those companies either that are in an industry in which doing so is the norm[14] or in which the management has a particularly keen awareness of CSR. This means that there is still an inherent and significant bias in these measurements.

The inconsistencies found in the data from reports of CSR-reporting companies are even more problematic. These often voluntarily reported CSR data will typically be operationally scoped (see the explanation at p. 36), i.e. the data will be unrelated to the financial results. Therefore, one cannot expect any correlation between financial performance and CSR reports, as the comparison is effectively between apples and oranges. Moreover, the data on the various overarching environmental themes or social measurements are not comparable across companies, or time for that matter, because the indicators are different – and even when they are the same, they are defined differently.

One has to wonder all the more what CSR analysis and rating agencies actually measure, rate, and index. Since their ratings and indices often comprise the basic data for the analysis and research carried out to prove or reject a possible link between CSR and financial performance, it is important for analysts to keep in mind a number of criticisms of those data sets, before they begin to use a given CSR rating index in their analyses.

The first point that analysts should consider is how the so-called Socially Responsible Investing (SRI) indices are screened, i.e. the selection method the agency uses to decide which companies it will allow to be included in its index. Basically, whether the companies are screened at all in itself entails a fairly big bias, but it is indeed the case that screening is often done.[15]

•   *Negative screening*: certain industries are often excluded from SRI indices. For example, rather large American investment funds of more or less religious origins exist, which call themselves SRI funds and screen for investments in companies that are involved in the following:

- o contraception
- o biotechnology
- o games
- o pornography
- o weapons
- o animal welfare.

Of course, SRI indices exist when these funds need this type of screening. The previously mentioned and often scientifically used KLD index[16] negatively screens companies involved in alcohol, gambling, tobacco, weapons, nuclear energy, pornography, and genetically modified products. Seen from a more secular Scandinavian perspective, one might view these selection criteria as odd. For example, Carlsberg and Zealand Pharma would be screened out because they produce beer and genetically modified products, respectively, while banks that lure customers to buy financial products of a chancy nature, which in recent years have brought families and companies into financial difficulties, are not screened out because the screening criteria used by the SRI indices do not equate chancy bank affairs with gambling. This, at least, is food for thought.

- *Positive screening*: companies are screened positively on the basis of their activities and/or what they disclose information about, for example, corporate governance, employee diversity, the environment, human rights, renewable energy, and CSR reporting. This means that companies are only included in the index if they meet certain criteria that have been determined as important. The limits to the criteria for inclusion are often not publicly available.[17] However, as opposed to the negatively screened index, this type of index includes significantly more innovative companies and pioneers in CSR.
- *Best in class*: this type of screening divides companies into industries or groups, and then evaluates their CSR performance compared with competitors that are deemed to have the same basic underlying conditions in their business. This is a slightly more inclusive method than the previous two, as it can (but not necessarily does) relate to all kinds of businesses. It is not apparent, however, how these screenings treat conglomerates, or whether there are certain industries that continue to be excluded.

All three forms of screening cause a significant bias in the analyses that are based on such SRI indices. It is of course also true that just because the company scores well in the rating (regardless of the screening method), it is not certain that it is beneficial to society or the world – it is so only a priori.

Often these SRI indices also include a bias towards large companies, as only very few small or medium-sized companies are found in these lists. Thus, in 2004, Hawken[18] showed that out of the 30 largest companies on the Dow Jones Industrial Average as of 30 December 2003, two-thirds were also on the list of the 30 most frequent investment objects of SRI investment funds – and over 90 percent of all Fortune 500 companies were to be found in one or more SRI funds. This may also explain the previously identified point that there is almost no correlation between a company's financial results and its CSR rating. Part of the explanation for this focus on large companies arises from the fact that most indices do not work with absolute data, but with relative ratings of companies, and there is only room for a certain number of companies in the index. Thus, there is no room for a small company that no one has heard of, regardless of how good it is at producing non-polluting perpetual-motion machines. In these relative indices, companies are often simply rated on home-made scales, for example, from CCC to AAA. In order to arrive at a rating on such a scale, rating agencies often assess solely whether a company measures and reports on a variety of indicators, a number of which are qualitative – as with the GRI rating in G3.[19] In addition, the different indicators are weighted differently in the different indices. This means that the development of the data or the data size in relation to the production of the company has less impact on the rating – if any. This would equate to financial rating agencies rating corporate financial potential based on whether the companies measure and report on their liabilities, intangible assets, and depreciation – and whether they have policies around these – instead of developing these data against production. It is probably unimaginable that any financial rating agency would be praised for doing so.

Finally, there is a bias relating to how agencies obtain the data for their analyses. Some rating agencies do not use company CSR reports, but instead send their own surveys[20] to companies, creating problems of bias concerning response rates and stratification of these data, as some companies are more likely than others to respond to such surveys; these kinds of survey data are not audited/reviewed, so their quality can probably be called into question too.

Despite all the deficiencies in these ratings and indices, they are widely used both as a basis for investment and for research and analysis of the financial performance of CSR. What is missing is a true index of all companies, which are rated on the same indicators, which are defined and consolidated in the same manner, and which are validated externally. Only then would it be possible to measure the actual impact of a company's CSR profile on its financial performance.

Conclusion

The conclusion of this review of whether CSR pays off is that we know nothing definite about whether CSR affects the profitability of a company. What we do know with some certainty is that CSR reporting can ensure more stable share prices – undoubtedly because CSR reporting creates a form of "insurance", such that any negative impact on share prices from adverse events is reduced. This is believed to be due to CSR reports providing investors with a greater insight into a company's risk profile, causing investors to respond less strongly to negative events. We can also have a legitimate expectation that institutional investors in particular are better able to use CSR reports to forecast a company's worth, creating lower capital costs for the company undertaking the CSR reporting – again probably because the investor can have a better understanding of the company's risk profile. Finally, we have also revised the logic of the success criteria of the CSR business case: maybe it is not so much about whether CSR is profitable, but rather whether not undertaking CSR is detrimental – especially for large, visible companies. Goldman Sachs had already indicated this in 2009:

> Despite disclosure and consistency challenges, ESG[21] performance has become sufficiently widespread that its analysis is valuable to long-term investors across all sectors. The number of companies whose performances we can measure with reported data is large enough to allow differentiation and non-reporting can provide an indication of the importance companies attach to ESG issues. However, more widespread disclosure across companies and reporting on a wider range of issues, on a consistent basis, will be key to ensuring investors are able to fully assess the effectiveness with which companies are addressing [the] breadth of issues facing their industries.[22]

Notes

1   Orlitzky *et al.* (2003).
2   Brammer *et al.* (2006).
3   Margolis *et al.* (2009).
4   Knox & Maklan (2004).

5   For example, Ali *et al.* (2010), Ferreira *et al.* (2010) or Hull and Rothenberg (2008).

6   Dhaliwal *et al.* (2011).

7   KLD (formerly known as Kinder Lyderberg Domini Research & Analytics) is one of the most-cited and used CSR rating agencies (Vogel 2006). More about KLD will follow.

8   Wang *et al.* (2011).

9   In 2008, China experienced a large food safety incident, when it was discovered that milk powder for infants and small children also contained melamine, a plastic used in the milk powder to increase the apparent protein content. Consuming melamine causes kidney malfunctions. More than 300,000 cases were later reported by the authorities, of which approximately 52,000 were hospitalized and six died ((BBC News, 24 November 2009: http://news.bbc.co.uk/2/hi/asia-pacific/8375638.stm (last accessed 22 February 2014).

10 Ioannou & Serafeim (2011).

11 Flammer (2012).

12 Barnea & Rubin (2010).

13 ACCA (2008), p. 6.

14 Typically companies in the medical, extractive, or retail industries, i.e. there are industries in which there is a significant probability that the companies' social or environmental impacts are not negligible, hence the expectations, at least in Europe, that the company will produce a CSR report. For example, there are not many carpet manufacturers or film producers that are known for their CSR initiatives and reporting. Thus, there is a major industry bias when conducting this type of analysis.

15 Hawken (2004).

16 MSCI KLD 400 Social Index's own description: http://www.msci.com/resources/factsheets/index_fact_sheet/msci-kld-400-social-index.pdf (last accessed 14 January 2014).

17 BertelsmannStiftung (2006).

18 Hawken (2004).

19 GRI: Global Reporting Initiative, G3: Generation 3. G4 was published in 2013. GRI, G3 allowed organizations to declare the use of the GRI in three levels – A, B, and C – where C is a simple report with ten indicators from the GRI list, and B is a moderate report that includes at least 20 indicators. Finally, level A is a report with all the GRI indicators. See also Chapter 3 "Rules and guidelines that exist" for more details and discussion about this level-indicator of reporting simply by counting the number of indicators.

20 Chatterji & Levine (2005).

21 ESG: Environmental, Social and corporate Governance.

22 Goldman Sachs (2009), p. 2.

3

RULES AND GUIDELINES THAT EXIST

Today, there is almost no legislation in the area of CSR; in contrast, there is a myriad of directions and guidelines, some of which are very good but others are so vague that they are close to being more misleading than instructive. Some guides also contradict each other, so a company must choose up front what it should lean on. The development of significant global rules and guidelines is broadly described in a historical context in Table 3.1.

TABLE 3.1 Historical development of CSR initiatives, regulations, and guidelines[a]

Year	Development
1976	The *OECD Guidelines for Multinational Enterprises* were released (OECD 1976); they were revised in 2011, when the *UN Guiding Principles on Business and Human Rights* (UN 2011) were also incorporated into a revised set of *OECD Guidelines for Multinational Enterprises* (OECD 2011)
1987	The UN published the "Brundtland Report" (*Our Common Future*), which contains 22 principles for future legislation that will help to ensure sustainability (UN 1987)
1997	The Global Reporting Initiative (GRI) was established, and the GRI released the first *Reporting Guidelines* in 2000; the fourth generation of the GRI was released in 2013 (GRI 2013)
2000	The UN Global Compact (UNGC) was prepared in 1999 and released in 2000; the UNGC LEAD was released in 2011
2000	The Carbon Disclosure Project was established to encourage companies to report their greenhouse gas (GHG) emissions
2001	The Greenhouse Gas Protocol (GHG protocol): *A Corporate Accounting and Reporting Standard* was published (WRI 2001)
2003	The *AccountAbility AA1000 Series of Standards* was released, and was subsequently revised and expanded in 2008 and 2011(ISEA 2011)

(Continued)

TABLE 3.1 (Continued)

Year	Development
2005	The UN invited different stakeholders to develop the *Principles for Responsible Investments* (PRI), which were released in 2006 (UNEP & UNGC 2006); in 2011, the *Principles for Investors in Inclusive Finance (PIIF)* were established (UNPRI *et al.* 2011); in 2012 the reporting was remodelled (UNPRI *et al.* 2012) and from 2013–14 it includes a second track for PIIF
2005	The International Organization for Standardization was initiated to establish a standard for social responsibility; in 2010, the first CSR standard, *ISO 26000*, was released (ISO 2010)
2010	The GRI and UNGC signed a memo showing commitment to combining their two initiatives
2011	The International Integrated Reporting Council (IIRC) prepared a discussion paper for integrated reporting with a variety of stakeholders; the framework was released in 2013
2012	XBRL International in collaboration with Deloitte established the first GRI taxonomy; a collaboration between XBRL International, the Climate Disclosure Project (CDP), the Climate Disclosure Standards Board (CDSB), and Fujitsu developed a taxonomy for GHG reporting
2013	The International Accounting Standards Board (IASB) and the IIRC signed a Memorandum of Understanding

a Inspired by Maguire (2011)

There are hundreds[1] of more or less global initiatives that a company can choose to join. Often these initiatives are derived from international conventions or make direct or indirect references to them. Some initiatives deal specifically with a theme, apply to a specific geographical area, or contain industry-related information. The initiatives presented in this book, however, are only the broad international initiatives that all companies can use and that are more common than most:

- OECD Guidelines for Multinational Enterprises
- United Nations Global Compact (UNGC)
- ISO 26000
- Greenhouse Gas (GHG) Protocol Initiative
- Global Reporting Initiative (GRI)
- AA1000 Series
- ISAE 3000
- International Integrated Reporting Council (IIRC)
- Principles for Responsible Investments (PRI).

None of the initiatives are legislative, but are only indicative of the direction in which local law and global practice may be moving.[2] These initiatives are presented in this chapter.

OECD Guidelines for Multinational Enterprises[3]

These guidelines are among the very first and date from 1976. Their purpose is to describe how a multinational company can work in harmony with local practice and ensure sustainable economic growth. The guidelines consist of a series of recommendations from OECD countries to multinational companies, and since they are only recommendations, they are inherently neither mandatory nor binding for the member states or companies. However, one of their strengths is that they are supported by both employers' and workers' organizations.

The guidelines consist of fairly comprehensive themes:

- employees' rights
- environment
- bribes
- consumer rights
- science and technology
- competition
- taxation.

In 2011, the OECD guidelines were reviewed, as a result of which they now have an increased focus on business and human rights. The guidelines are though rather weak both in the definition of how they should be fulfilled as well as in the follow-up on the part of the OECD on whether companies are in compliance with them. OECD countries have national focal points, and the plan is for them to be strengthened in the coming years. The guidelines also form the basis of a number of recent guidelines, including the much greater and better-known UNGC.

United Nations Global Compact (UNGC)[4]

These guidelines are certainly the world's most widely used among the international guidelines, with participation from over 10,000 companies and organizations globally.[5] The guidelines were developed by John Ruggie at the United Nations (UN) in 1999 under the leadership of Kofi Annan, and launched in 2000. Like the OECD guidelines, the UNGC is not mandatory, but the UN follows up the companies joining the UNGC to ensure that they actually make and submit a progress report as required (a Communication on Progress (COP)) – a requirement that was introduced in 2003.[6] However, how the companies act in reality and what the COP must include more specifically are somewhat more weakly defined, although there are a number of general criteria that must be met in order for a report to be accepted as a COP:

- a statement by the company's CEO in which he or she declares his or her continued support for the initiative and the ten principles (see Table 3.2)
- a description of the practical initiatives that the company has taken or plans to take to implement the ten principles covering the four themes (see Table 3.2). If one or more themes are not covered in the COP, an explanation should be provided (the report or explain principle – however, this only takes effect five years after the company has joined the UNGC). There is no requirement for the COP to contain all ten principles, as the company should prioritize according to its core business
- measurements of the implication of the company's business as such and the outcome of the initiatives undertaken. The extent to which objectives made previously have been achieved should also be apparent.

The COP must be forwarded every year to the Global Compact website:

- A company subscribing to the UNGC must submit its first COP within 12 months – and from then on following COPs must also be submitted within 12 months of each other. This requirement could mean that the company might need to apply for permission from the UN to report at different times from one year to the next; given that the COP is supposed to be published together with the annual report (which is mandatory in some countries), this situation could arise if the company's annual report release is somewhat movable.

A questionnaire must also be completed in connection with the submission of the COP. The UN instigates sanctions against those companies that do not publish a COP under these rules or for which the COP cannot be approved. The sanction is that they are removed from the list of signatories, which the especially interested can find on the UN website.[7]

The UNGC's purpose is to contribute to a solution to the challenge of globalization, and includes ten principles divided into four themes (see Table 3.2).

TABLE 3.2 UNGC's ten principles

Human Rights	Principle 1: Businesses should support and respect the protection of internationally proclaimed human rights
	Principle 2: Businesses should make sure that they are not complicit in human rights abuses
Labour	Principle 3: Businesses should uphold the freedom of association and the effective recognition of the right to collective bargaining
	Principle 4: Businesses should support the elimination of all forms of forced and compulsory labour
	Principle 5: Businesses should uphold the effective abolition of child labour
	Principle 6: Businesses should eliminate discrimination in respect of employment and occupation
Environment	Principle 7: Businesses should support a precautionary approach to environmental challenges
	Principle 8: Businesses should undertake initiatives to promote greater environmental responsibility
	Principle 9: Businesses should encourage the development and diffusion of environmentally friendly technologies
Anti-corruption	Principle 10: Businesses should work against all forms of corruption, including extortion and bribery

www.unglobalcompact.org/abouttheGC/TheTenPrinciples/index.html (last accessed 14 January 2014)

The ten principles are all based on UN conventions, which give them a global nature that is easy to communicate to companies.[8] The UNGC has never intended to work with these principles as actual legislative regulations, but they should be complementary to the conventions. This is partly because the primary aim of the UNGC is to create dialogue, and not to serve as a code or a verification system, but probably also because the UN has neither the mandate nor the resources to follow up on what companies/organizations actually do.

ISO 26000[9]

ISO 26000 is a standard that supervises the areas that CSR should address, how companies define stakeholders, how companies should deal with stakeholders, and especially how far companies' responsibilities extend. The standard should, in other words, constitute a major contribution to defining the boundaries to CSR reports, though ISO 26000 is aimed not only at companies but also at, for instance, non-profit organizations and therefore on purpose refers to SR – without the "corporate" part.

The standard was released in 2010 and has been prepared with participation from more than 90 countries, including experts representing everything from authorities, employees, consumers, NGOs, etc. A company cannot be ISO 26000 certified – the standard works more as a guideline. However, some countries have established national standards against which organizations can be certified: for example, Denmark has ISO 26001,[10] which is structured like ISO 9001 for quality management and ISO 14001 for environmental management, but naturally contains topics from ISO 26000.

ISO 26000 contains seven key subjects, each of which contains one to eight standards (clauses):

- organizational governance
- human rights
- labour practice
- the environment
- fair operating practices
- consumer issues
- local community involvement and development.

According to ISO 26000, an organization/company is required to relate to all seven key subjects before it can call itself socially responsible. The way in which a company can use ISO 26000 is to incorporate the standard into existing ISO certifications, which can enable the company to maintain its certifications, while at the same time promoting sustainability. The alternative is to apply any national standards, such as the Danish standards, to obtain certification.

Greenhouse Gas (GHG) Protocol Initiative[11]

The GHG Protocol is a voluntary, international accounting and reporting standard that should enable companies and organizations to quantify GHG emissions of different types in the same way. The protocol is widely used both in connection with voluntary and statutory reports and when trading CO_2 emissions or imposing carbon taxes. One of the main features of the GHG Protocol is that it has defined three so-called scopes, which are to be used when a company measures, quantifies, and reports CO_2 and CO_2 equivalents:

- *Scope 1*: direct emissions resulting from the company's own consumption of fuels and gases
- *Scope 2*: indirect emissions resulting from the energy used to produce electricity and/or heating power, which the company has purchased for its use
- *Scope 3*: indirect emissions from third-party activities related to the company's value chain, including customers and suppliers and outsourced services and activities.

Most companies only measure scopes 1 and 2,[12] and particularly advanced companies incorporate scope 3 to the extent that it is feasible and beneficial to the understanding of the companies' production. If all companies used this division in the same way, then it would be possible for the UN to calculate the actual CO_2 emissions in the whole world without double-counting, by merely adding up the scope 1 emissions. Unfortunately, the protocol is ambiguous in its definitions and the accompanying guidelines. Thus, when some choose to interpret the model differently from others, they are probably not breaking the protocol, but the UN will have difficulties in using their contributions in a master equation. All other companies/organizations will also have trouble using these companies/organizations' CO_2 reporting for benchmarking, just as the odd reporting company/organization will have trouble finding a suitable context for its reporting (see also "Financial vs operational boundaries" on p. 36).

Global Reporting Initiative (GRI)[13]

The GRI is a voluntary initiative established in the US in 1997 by the Coalition for Environmentally Responsible Economies (Ceres) and the Tellus Institute with support from the UN Environment Programme (UNEP); the GRI is almost as prevalent as the UNGC.[14] The idea was and is to create an international framework of principles and standard indicators, which could be used by companies when producing a CSR report. The GRI has developed over time, and in 2013 launched the fourth generation of the framework: G4.

G4 defines ten principles: four for the content of the report and six for its quality. The four principles for the content of the report comprise:[15]

- *Stakeholder inclusiveness*: the organization should identify its stakeholders and explain how it has responded to their reasonable expectations and interests.

- *Sustainability context*: the report should present the organization's performance in the wider context of sustainability.
- *Materiality*: the report should cover aspects that reflect the organization's significant economic, environmental, and social impacts or that substantively influence the assessments and decisions of stakeholders.
- *Completeness*: the report should include coverage of material aspects and their boundaries, sufficient to reflect significant economic, environmental, and social impacts and to enable stakeholders to assess the organization's performance in the reporting period.

The six principles for quality read:

- *Balance*: the report should reflect positive and negative aspects of the organization's performance.
- *Comparability*: the organization should select, compile, and report information consistently. The reported information should be presented in a manner that enables stakeholders to analyse changes in the organization's performance over time and that could support analysis relative to other organizations.
- *Accuracy*: the reported information should be sufficiently accurate and detailed for stakeholders to assess the organization's performance.
- *Timeliness*: the organization should report on a regular schedule so that information is available in time for stakeholders to make informed decisions.
- *Clarity*: the organization should make information available in a manner that is understandable and accessible to stakeholders using the report.
- *Reliability*: the organization should gather, record, compile, analyze, and disclose information and processes used in the preparation of a report in such a way that they can be subject to examination and that establishes the quality and materiality of the information.

Thus, the GRI has quality principles similar to those in the annual financial report, but the way of choosing the content is considerably different. For example, "reliability" is financially weighted at least as highly as "relevance" (in the GRI defined by the first four content principles – in the following called materiality), if not higher. This means that in the preparation of a financial report the company may well be in a situation in which it has relevant information, but the information fails to meet the requirement of reliability, so it cannot be published. "It is obvious that the information must be reliable before it is sufficiently credible to make economic decisions based on it".[16] In the GRI, it is only materiality that is superior to the other concepts. This logic is probably not appropriate for an investor.

G4 is being phased in during 2014 and 2015, and companies can continue to use the old version G3/G3.1. G3 was used in several ways – either as a fully comprehensive reporting framework or simply as guidelines and inspiration. G3 allowed organizations to declare the use of the GRI in three levels – A, B, and C – where C is a simple report with ten indicators from the GRI list, as minimum economic, social, and environmental data; and B is a moderate report that includes at least 20 indicators covering economics, environment, human rights, labour, society, and product responsibility. Finally, level A is a report in full compliance with the GRI indicators covering:

- environment
- human rights
- labour
- society
- product liability
- economy.

The levels were said not to be a quality indicator, but this is difficult to communicate to non-CSR experts. Furthermore, organizations can then themselves put a "+" at the end of the self-declared A, B, or C level, if the report (or parts of the report) is verified by a third party or if the company has its report verified by the GRI before publishing. Regardless of the verification method (or no verification), if the organization wants to incorporate a GRI application-level indicator into the report, then it has to forward it to the GRI as either hard or soft copy.

G3 has been much criticized for many reasons (see also Chapter 4 "Rules that ought to exist"), but especially because of this layout using levels: simply counting the number of indicators has not exactly been conducive to the principle about materiality (with or without the limitations this principle has otherwise), as the number of indicators says nothing about the quality of the data. G4 was developed in light of these criticisms, but in reality the levelling has not been eliminated. Although G4 has rightly removed the A to C levels, they have simply been replaced with two reporting options: core and comprehensive. Specific standard disclosures have been defined, which comprise disclosures on the management approach and indicators, and which cover:

- strategy and analysis
- organizational profile

- identified material aspects and boundaries
- stakeholder engagement
- report profile
- governance
- ethics and integrity
- general standard disclosures for sectors (required, if available for the organization's sector; what is required for conglomerates is not mentioned).

To be reporting in accordance with core disclosure, at least one indicator related to each identified material aspect needs to be included; if the reporting is comprehensible, then the report has to cover all the indicators related to each identified material aspect, though there could be omissions in exceptional cases. In these cases, the report should clearly:

- identify the information that has been omitted
- explain the reasons why the information has been omitted.

The explanation has to be one of the following:

- a standard disclosure, part of a standard disclosure, or an indicator are not applicable; the reason why these or one of them is considered to be not applicable should be disclosed
- the information is subject to specific confidentiality constraints; these constraints are to be disclosed by the organization
- the existence of specific legal prohibitions; a reference to the specific legal prohibitions should be made
- the information is currently unavailable; in this case, the organization should disclose the steps being taken to obtain the data and the expected time frame for doing so.

If the organization has a large number of omitted standard disclosures, this may invalidate its ability to claim that its sustainability report has been prepared "in accordance" with either the core or the comprehensive option of the guidelines.

This treatment of omissions is particularly strange when seen from a financial point of view – it would never be allowed financially. Imagine that the International Financial Reporting Standards (IFRS) would allow a company not to depreciate or write down its assets, because "the information is currently unavailable": that, of course, would not happen.

The GRI G4 defines a very wide array of indicators, but in reality the definitions are very imprecise: for example, does the total number of employees (G4-9) refer to full-time equivalents (FTEs) or headcounts (HC), and is it on average or at year-end, and how should employees on leave be treated, not to mention employees leased in and out? These issues are discussed in greater detail in Chapter 5 "Proposed minimum data".

AA1000 Series – especially AA1000AS[17]

The Institute of Social and Ethical AccountAbility (often referred to simply as "AccountAbility", and which applies the abbreviation "AA" to its series of standards) was founded in 1996 and operates as a non-profit organization. It has released the AA1000 Series, which also contains a suggestion for a review standard. The AA1000 is a series of three standards:

- *The AA1000 AccountAbility Principles Standard (APS)*: a framework for companies and organizations to identify, prioritize, and respond to CSR challenges. The APS provides three basic principles that a company must adhere to in order to put the AA1000 logo on its CSR report, these being involvement, materiality, and responsiveness.
- *The AA1000 Assurance Standard (AS)*: a standard for accountants and other CSR reviewers, which is used to evaluate the extent to which an organization is in compliance with the AA1000APS, whereby a stakeholder approach is ensured.
- *The AA1000 Stakeholder Engagement Standard (SES)*: a framework to help companies and organizations ensure that they have performed a stakeholder engagement process that is purpose-driven, robust, and delivers results.

The AA1000AS 2008 has two types of assurance: a type of compliance with the principles of the APS (type 1) and a type that also incorporates the reliability of the data (type 2). The idea of this division is that companies can choose to have their observance of principles reviewed each year, while data validation can be performed less often, which should reduce the review costs. This is an idea that is probably not exactly comprehensible to the investor: if/when CSR data become incorporated into the investment analysis, he or she will be reliant on data validity and completeness.

The AA1000AS also has two levels of validation: moderate and high. The idea of this division is that it must be possible for companies that are less mature in CSR reporting to choose initially only to have a moderate-level validation, and then later to choose a high level. Companies can also choose to have selected parts of the report at a high review level, while the remainder are at a moderate level. AccountAbility claims that this should ensure comparability across companies – it can be a little hard for investors to follow this logic.

A conclusion that is based on the moderate level of assurance does appear to be mainly based on evidence found internally at a company's corporate level and only to a very limited extent further down in the organization. The evidence requirements extend only to interviews, an overall analysis, and a very limited amount of substantive review. The requirement of proof is only plausibility – not reliability. Therefore, the conclusion is also limited by the actions that are actually undertaken, which therefore also have to be described in the review statement.

In contrast, the conclusion of a statement based on a high level of assurance will require evidence gathered from both internal and external sources; in particular, the requirement covers all the layers of the organization. The evidence requirements also include a substantive review, as the concluding section also deals with the reliability of the information published.

An AA1000AS statement is an evaluation of the report regarding inclusivity, materiality, and responsiveness in relation to the stakeholders. The form of the statement is an expanded, detailed description of the issues that the auditor/reviewer has found during the review and any advice for the future – often the issues that in the financial world would be found in a management letter, which is not published externally. This statement form is thus considerably different from a financial statement, which is given a special shape with standard content, whereby the reader can immediately assess whether there is a so-called "blank endorsement" or not, and very quickly evaluate the report's quality. It is considerably more difficult with an AA1000 statement to assess immediately the quality of the report; this may give rise to some misunderstandings, especially by financial experts who may not be very familiar with CSR, and who sometimes have problems understanding these often very extensive statements, which almost always include one or more criticisms – such statements are rare in the financial world.

ISAE 3000[18]

The ISAE 3000 is an international standard for issuance of statements of non-financial reports, which the International Federation of Accountants (IFAC) is behind. Only members of the IFAC are allowed to make statements according to this standard, i.e. the classic auditors.

The ISAE 3000 is a standard that in part requires the auditor to consider three principal questions before he assumes the review task, these being:

- Has the company implemented the necessary quality process?
- Does the review team have the necessary professional qualifications?
- Can the auditor code of conduct be applied?

However, the standard also involves a number of requirements concerning the level of understanding, which the auditor must have achieved in order to make a statement. Since the ISAE 3000 is subject to the general conceptual framework for audits, the review of the non-financial report must be based on evidence. Such evidence might aptly be defined pursuant to the ISA 500 standard, i.e. it shall be sufficient, suitable, and reliable evidence for the auditor to draw conclusions. Sufficiency deals with the amount of evidence, suitability deals with the quality of the evidence, and reliability is affected by the source and nature of the evidence. General rules for assessing the weaknesses of the financial evidence can therefore be of great benefit when also applied to non-financial data[19] if the ISAE 3000 is used (see Figure 3.1).

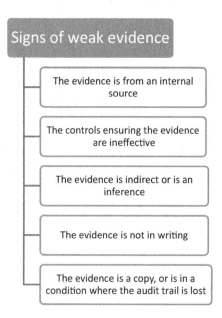

FIGURE 3.1   Signs of weak evidence

If there are signs of weakness in the evidence, the auditor must collect more evidence, preferably using different methods and/or from different sources, in order to increase the assurance of the content, which can then form the basis of a statement with the desired assurance.

The auditor must, when planning the review, evaluate the task, partly defining the risk of the task and partly defining the materiality level. The risk of the task is related to whether the auditor is likely to reach a wrong conclusion. The risk may be linked to several factors:

- *Inherent risk*: the tendency for the data set to contain material misstatement
- *Control risk*: restrictions on the possible execution of internal controls in the company
- *Detection risk*: the probability that the auditor will not detect material misstatements.

Materiality is related to the auditor's assessment of which factors will add value for the users of the report and thus change the users' decisions. Often materiality will be a quantitative estimation, which is calculated as a percentage of other quantified measures, such as sales, total assets, production amounts or CO_2 emissions, etc. However, materiality can also be a qualitative estimation[20] – or it can be a combination of the two.

Hence, materiality as a concept is not the same in the ISAE 3000 as in the AA1000AS, but in both these standards it is based on the same logic.

> An issue, concern or impact is material if it could influence the decisions, actions and behaviour of stakeholders or the organisation itself. The AA1000 Assurance Standard, by recognising stakeholders as users and by requiring that stakeholders in the determination of materiality makes it clear that they are an important source of evidence and that their views count in the determination of materiality.[21]

The big difference between ISAE 3000 and AA1000AS is in their treatment of stakeholders. Stakeholders do not need to be involved when a company is making an ISAE 3000 statement, but they can be if the company combines the AA1000AS and the ISAE 3000 type 2 statements. When the company uses the ISAE 3000, it is assumed that the users of the report, and the indicators to be reported on, have already been defined.[22] Thus, essentially an ISAE 3000 statement on its own is related to these predefinitions, and therefore not open to all possible indicators; however, openness to a wide range of indicators might be regarded by some stakeholders as essential, and indeed it is integral to the AA1000AS statement.

Just as with the AA1000AS, the ISAE 3000 has two levels of assurance: limited or reasonable. For the auditor making a statement, there are two main differences between these levels. First, a statement with limited assurance is negative, while a statement with reasonable assurance is positive; in the latter case the auditor must therefore positively confirm something in his or her conclusion. Second, in the case of limited assurance, the auditor need not seek further evidence when faced with weak evidence, unless it conflicts with another source of data; in contrast, reasonable assurance has to be based on strong evidence. The conceptual framework for the auditor does not operate to quantify the probability of reaching a wrong conclusion, but the practice is that it is assumed that a statement of reasonable assurance is an expression that the conclusion is 90–95 percent sure, whereas a statement with limited assurance does not have to be more than 50 percent sure.[23]

For the auditor to issue an ISAE 3000 statement, he or she is required to follow a systematic assignment process which includes:

- having an understanding of the subject matter and other conditions of the job, which often involves an understanding of the internal controls
- using this understanding to assess the risks that the subject matter could involve a material misstatement
- responding to the assessed risks, including a general reaction and determining the nature, timing, and extent of further work
- performing additional work that is clearly related to the identified risks, comprising a combination of:
  - examination
  - monitoring
  - confirmation
  - recalculation
  - repetition
  - analytical procedures
  - queries
  - testing of controls
- assessing the evidence's adequacy and suitability.

In addition, the auditor must obtain a management statement and consider the effects of subsequent events on both the data set and the auditor's report until the report is made, as well as obtain evidence to prove the statement. If the auditor becomes aware of issues that should be communicated to the company management during the review actions, he or she will also need to consider whether a report or a letter to the board and/or management of the undertaking organization must be made. As shown, the ISAE 3000 is a much more solid form of review than that of the AA1000AS. For the investor, it is a guarantee that the review is carried out uniformly between several investment objects, so the statements and thus the reports are supposed to be comparable immediately, especially if the recipients of the reporting are defined as being the same, and the indicators being reported on are the same. By contrast, the rules for operating with two levels of assurance for statements do not help the investor, regardless of whether the AA1000AS or the ISAE 3000 is used; this most likely creates more confusion than clarity and comparability between reports.

International Integrated Reporting Council (IIRC)[24]

In 2009, HRH The Prince of Wales convened a high-level meeting of investors, standard setters, companies, accounting bodies, and UN representatives to establish the IIRC, a body to oversee the creation of a globally accepted International Integrated Reporting Framework. The IIRC is the global authority on integrated reporting: <IR>. Its mission is to enable integrated reporting to be embedded into mainstream business practice in the public and private sectors. In December 2013, the International <IR> Framework was published based on feedback from a hearing exercise on a draft made in spring 2013. Thus, we have yet to see how many companies will actually use this framework.

The framework has seven guiding principles:

- *Strategic focus and future orientation*
- *Connectivity of information*: the report should provide a holistic picture of the combination, interrelatedness, and dependencies to create value over time
- *Stakeholder relationships*: reminiscent of the GRI methodology (see p. 18)
- *Materiality*: reminiscent of the GRI definition
- *Conciseness*
- *Reliability and completeness*: all material matters, both positive and negative, should be included (reminiscent of the GRI's demands for a balanced report)
- *Consistency and comparability*: a base-year should be defined for comparison and to ensure comparability with other organizations to the extent that it is material to create value over time.

The framework does not prescribe specific key performance indicators or measurement methods, but it does include a small number of requirements that are to be applied before an integrated report can be said to be in accordance with the framework. An integrated report aims to provide insights into the resources and relationships used and affected by an organization – these are called "the capitals". The capitals are stocks of value that are increased, decreased, or transformed through the activities and outputs of the organization, which also can cause an outcome/impact subsequently.[25] Six capitals are mentioned in the framework, though the company is not required to exactly adopt the categorization or structure for the report along the lines of these capitals, and as indicated, the measurement methodology of these capitals is not defined either:

- financial capital
- manufactured capital
- intellectual capital
- human capital
- social and relational capital
- natural capital.

Furthermore, the integrated report must include eight content elements:

- *Organizational overview and external environment*: what does the organization do and under which circumstances?
- *Governance*: and how does this structure support the value in the short, medium, and long term?
- *Business model*
- *Risks and opportunities*: what affects the organization's ability to create value over the short, medium, and long term and how does the organization deal with these risks and opportunities?
- *Strategy and resource allocation*: where to go and how?
- *Performance*: has the organization achieved its strategic objectives and what are the outcomes in terms of effects on the capitals?
- *Outlook*: what are the challenges and uncertainties for future performance?
- *Basis of presentation*: how does the organization determine which issues to include in the report?

In 2013 the International Accounting Standards Board (IASB) and the IIRC signed a Memorandum of Understanding,[26] as a result of which this new framework ought to be of greater interest to the regular financial reporters – it is now more likely than ever that in the future the IFRS will be driving towards integrated reporting. So far, however, the IASB has not launched any projects involving integrated reporting – the closest is the fairly small IASB project on how to report emission trading schemes.[27]

Principles for Responsible Investments (PRI)[28]

The PRI is an initiative within the UN framework, which intends to ensure that institutional investors, investment banks, and investment advisors relate to sustainability when investing. As with the UNGC, the PRI is a voluntary scheme, which the investor can choose to sign and adhere to and to file an annual report with. The PRI currently has 1,227 members,[29] of which 275 are asset owners.

Investors who have endorsed the PRI are obliged to follow six principles and report on their work in accordance with these principles:

* The investor will incorporate environmental, social, and active ownership into investment analysis and decisions.
* The investor will be an active owner and incorporate ESG issues into policies concerning ownership and the practical management of investments.
* The investor will seek appropriate disclosure on environmental, social, and active ownership of the units invested in.
* The investor will promote acceptance and implementation of the principles within the investment industry.
* The investor will cooperate in order to increase efficiency in implementing the principles.
* The investor will report on activities and progress towards implementing the principles.

The reporting was divided into 12 modules from 2013, but as a rule of thumb, it will only be mandatory to complete a module if signatories have 10 percent or more of their assets under management in that asset class, but they can of course report voluntarily on more modules. Within each module there is a wide range of indicators, some of which are mandatory to report and disclose and some which are voluntary, and finally some that are mandatory to report but voluntary to disclose. The modules are:[30]

* *Module OO*: Organizational Overview
* *Module OA*: Overarching Approach

- *Module SAM*: Manager Selection, Appointment, and Monitoring
- *Module LEI*: Listed Equity Incorporation
- *Module LEA*: Listed Equity Active Ownership
- *Module PE*: Private Equity
- *Module PR*: Property
- *Module IFD*: Inclusive Finance Direct
- *Module IFI*: Inclusive Finance Indirect
- *Module CM*: Closing Module
- *Module FI*: Fixed Income
- *Module INF*: Infrastructure.

Unfortunately, most of the mandatory indicators to report and disclose are somewhat vague, and relate mostly to which rules the investment company has written, but not how they are enforced. One could, for example, easily have imagined a key figure à la (scope $1+2$ CO_2e)/investor-dollar, which all public PRI reports should contain, but that requirement does not exist. If the requirement had existed, we would probably have seen significantly more robust reporting requirements from institutional investors for their investment objects' CSR reporting.

From the 2013/2014 reporting cycle, the reporting has to be made via an online tool and disclose a subset of these indicators on the PRI website. The idea behind this online tool is that there will be at least three outputs: Ready-Made Responsible Investment (RI) Transparency Reports, confidential Assessment Reports, and the annual Report on Progress.

The PRI has also established the Principles for Investors in Inclusive Finance (PIIF) in 2011.[31] The PIIF are housed within the PRI, wherefore signatories to the PIIF are also requested to sign the PRI. When signing the PIIF, investors commit to:

- expanding the range of financial services available to low-income people
- integrating client protection into all their policies and practices
- treating their investees fairly, with clear and balanced contracts and dispute resolution procedures
- integrating ESG factors into their policies and reporting
- promoting transparency in all their operations
- pursuing balanced long-term returns that reflect the interests of clients, retail providers, and end investors
- working together to develop common investor standards on inclusive finance.

PIIF signatories are obliged to report on modules IFD and IFI, while if they hold more than 50 percent of assets under management in IFD, they can choose not to report the OA module, but instead describe their approach in a specific indicator in this module.

How much are the guidelines used?

In the analysis made for this book of the Forbes 50 largest listed companies in the world, the percentage of companies that refer specifically to the guidelines are as follows:[32]

- OECD Guidelines for Multinational Enterprises = 16 percent
- UNGC = 42 percent
- ISO 26000 = 10 percent
- GHG Protocol Initiative = 54 percent (indirectly referenced, measured against whether the company reports GHGs in scopes)[12]
- GRI = 72 percent
- AA1000 series = 20 percent (90 percent of these are with low assurance)
- ISAE 3000 = 32 percent (87 percent of these are with low assurance)
- PRI = 72 percent (of the banking and investment companies).

Notes

1   Roepstorff & Serpa (2005).
2   See UNEP *et al.* (2013) for an overview of local and regional rules and guidelines.
3   Leipziger (2010).
4   Leipziger (2010); Mogensen *et al.* (2011); Schur et al. (2011); www.unglobal-compact.org
5   May 2013, www.unglobalcompact.org/participantsandstakeholders/
6   Hamid & Johner (2010).
7   www.unglobalcompact.org/docs/news_events/9.1_news_archives/2010_02_01/Delisted_Final_1Feb.pdf
8   The Universal Declaration of Human Rights, the ILO's Fundamental Principles on Rights at Work (ILO 1998), and the Rio Declaration on Environment and Development.
9   Leipziger (2010); www.iso.org/iso/home/standards/iso26000.htm
10   Also known as DS 49001: www.dscert.dk/da-DK/aktuelt/nyhedsarkiv/Sider/DS26001.aspx
11   www.ghgprotocol.org/about-ghgp

12 In the analysis made of the Forbes 50 largest listed companies' reporting, 54 percent report on scopes 1 and 2 – while scope 3 is only reported by 40 percent of the companies, often also only generated via employees' business travel and/or commuting. Full-circle environmental reporting on company products is only performed by 8 percent of companies, and 32 percent of the companies report on CO_2 without defining the scope, while 14 percent do not report on CO_2 emissions at all.

13 www.globalreporting.org/Pages/default.aspx

14 Of the Forbes 50 largest listed companies' reporting, 72 percent use the GRI as a reference, while only 42 percent refer specifically to the UNGC. This is very interesting compared with regular reporting – and it seems that the North American companies especially (which represent one-third of the 50 largest companies) prefer to refer to the GRI as a reporting guideline without the UNGC, whereas Asian and European companies refer to the UNGC twice as often as the North American companies do.

15 GRI (2013).

16 Jeppesen & Madsen (2011), p. 12.

17 ISEA (2011).

18 IAASB (2011).

19 Füchsel *et al.* (2005); Samuelsen (2007).

20 Collings (2011).

21 AccountAbility (2006), p. 15.

22 Iansen-Rogers & Oelschlaegel (2005).

23 Füchsel *et al.* (2005).

24 IIRC (2013).

25 See also Appendix G for a suggestion of an IIRC integrated note.

26 www.ifrs.org/use-around-the-world/Pages/IASB-and-IIRC-MoU.aspx

27 www.ifrs.org/Current-Projects/IASB-Projects/Emission-Trading-Schemes/Pages/Emissions-Trading-Schemes.aspx

28 www.unpri.org/

29 December 2013, www.unpri.org/signatories/signatories/

30 UNPRI (2013).

31 www.unpri.org/areas-of-work/piif/

32 The IIRC is kept outside the analysis, as it is completely new.

4

RULES THAT OUGHT TO EXIST

Having now gained an overview of all the non-judicial instructions or guidelines that have been developed during the last 30 years, it is time to ask – are these good enough if we want to ensure that investors can actually use CSR reports in their evaluation of corporate performance? To answer this question, we must examine what is required from CSR reports in order for them to be useful to investors. François Passant, Executive Director at EuroSif, puts it this way:

> A growing number of investors are taking extra-financial factors into account when making investment decisions…To further accelerate this growth, a couple of things need to happen, some of them being 'regulatory' some of them being behavioural. These include for instance:
>
> • the need to improve the conciseness, timeliness, comparability and materiality of corporate extra-financial reporting for investors
> • the need to progress further on the use and homogenization of core extra-financial KPIs across companies and/or sectors
> • the need to further clarify that fiduciary duty is a notion that is absolutely compatible with ESG…
> • the need to further train mainstream financial analysts on the materiality of extra-financial factors and foster a cultural change within these teams.[1]

Thus, it is clear that varieties of technical formalities, which have far-reaching consequences, still have not been put into place legislatively, and therefore have and will continue to have an impact on whether CSR data actually can or could be used by investors. The last point on culture change will be further considered later in this book – for now, let us focus on rules that ought to exist.

How can we ensure that CSR reports are useful to investors?

If CSR reporting is to be meaningful to investors, the various ways in which investors work must be clarified, which can determine whether data could possibly be involved in the analysis of investment objects.

- The data must be quantified. Investors do not read 80 pages of narrative and illustrations per company, when they are choosing between thousands of investment possibilities: "96% of investors agreed or strongly agreed that quantitative key performance indicators are essential to assess corporate sustainability performance."[2]
- The data must be standardized, so it is possible to compare companies and see development over time. Only then is it possible to assess a given company's financial and non-financial performance in relation to its production and market. Standards are the basis for valid investment choices: "To be useful in portfolio analysis, ESG reporting guidelines must define with a great degree of precision what companies should disclose and how they should disclose it, just as FASB[3] and other regulatory bodies specify how they must define financial factors such as profit, loss, revenue, and goodwill."[4]
- The data must be easily accessible. This means that there must be standards stating how the data are presented, their format, and not least in which media they are presented.[5]
- The data quality must be verifiable and should be of the same quality as financial data. Again, this requires the data to be standardized and well defined, so that the auditor has a chance of ensuring their validity and completeness: "…investors want assurance that this data is of high quality, as they want information that they can rely on for their decision-making."[6]

How are CSR data reported today? In the analysis[7] of the 50 largest listed companies in the world conducted for this book, it appears that reporting is certainly not standardized, data are often very difficult to access (if there are any quantitative data), and only 31 companies' CSR reports have been verified by an external auditor or other reviewer. Of the 50 companies, there is only one that does not report any CSR in any shape or form, but the rest do actually undertake some CSR reporting, either integrated into or combined with the annual report, on the Web or in a stand-alone report. CSR reporting is, in other words, by now quite mainstream, and one would expect it to be possible to demand a certain level of quality. However, of the 49 companies who do produce a CSR report, only 23 define their boundaries and consolidation methods – the remaining 26 companies report measurements without defining how these are made. The 23 companies, having defined their boundaries and consolidation methodologies, use different methods: some only include 100 percent owned subsidiaries and others include all their subsidiaries regardless of ownership, but not joint operations. Yet others use what is known as operational boundaries, which means that everything the company operates (but not necessarily owns) is included 100 percent, while omitting non-operated (but owned) activities. All these methods are currently legal, but have the caveat that they cause the CSR measurements to be without meaningful context as assessed against the financial data, since they do not use the same boundaries and consolidation rules as are used financially, i.e. according to the IFRS. CSR measurements are thus context-free, which results in figures that say nothing about anything – they are just numbers. Neither investors nor companies can use such data for much. Of the 23 boundary-defining companies, only three use boundaries that are related to financial data!

To ensure comparability between companies – but in fact also within each company – CSR data have to be made relative to production volumes, revenue, cash flow, etc. Thus, it is very important that the figures are consolidated, as happens financially. Similarly, it is vital that the boundaries for CSR reporting are in line with those that the companies use when producing financial data, known as financial boundaries. Such an approach would also be in full harmony with new legislation in the UK if using the CDSB-framework,[8] where all listed companies from 2013 are to report on their GHG emissions in their annual financial reports – and this should of course be executed with financial boundaries.[9]

For a financial analyst, this is clearly and deeply logical, but it is far from being so for all the CSR departments. The reason for this collision of logic is presumably that many companies have started reporting on CSR to various authorities,[10] who ask for safety reporting, green reports, and others for individual production locations (a farm, a factory, a building site, a drilling rig, a vessel, etc.). The authorities do not care who owns the production from the production site: they only want to receive a single report from each production site, which is received from the operator. Thus, some CSR departments have thought that if the company simply added together the regulatory reports they were responsible for making, then this would result in a real company CSR report. Such a report is produced within operational boundaries. Note also that operational boundaries are so poorly defined that even authorities and interest groups in the same country can follow different definitions of the boundaries – and across national borders there are even more definitions. This means that these simple summary reports are patchworks, in which definitions and consolidation are not harmonized at the company's corporate level. This would equate to a corporation adding up the financial statutory accounts 1+1+1, and not using IFRS standards and regulations to harmonize and normalize the data when consolidating. No financial person would ever dream of doing so. CSR departments thus have to accept that there can be many truths – some required for the local authorities under local laws, and using a variety of local definitions – but when a corporation reports CSR, there can be only one common set of rules. This is also the reality for financial reporting; financially, the legal company reports one thing to the authorities (statutory accounts), and it also reports a second set of data to the tax authorities given the tax laws, but when the data are to be consolidated into corporate reports, they have to follow the corporate rules.

Financial vs operational boundaries

The first issue that the CSR reporting company should figure out, when planning for the next CSR report, is which activities should be included and which should be omitted. As just indicated, there is still a very basic discussion to be had that often has two different outcomes, that is, whether the company reports following operational or financial boundaries:

- "Operational boundaries" is the definition the company uses when including data from all the activities it operates and omitting everything else.
- "Financial boundaries" is the definition the company uses when including data from all the activities contributing to the production, revenue, and cash flow of the company – regardless of whether it is operated by the company or not.

At first, these may sound like two relatively similar definitions, but that is not necessarily the case. There are at least two areas that can lead to very different data being used within a CSR report: leasing and joint operations.

Leasing

To understand the problem of leasing,[11] we have to start somewhere else. Overall, companies will measure CO_2 given the GHG Protocol's three scopes (see Chapter 3 "Rules and guidelines that exist"). The crux of this protocol is: when does the company have scope 1 consumption (i.e. direct consumption) of chemicals, fuels, and gases? The answer depends entirely on whether the company uses financial or operational boundaries. If the company uses financial boundaries, the logic is that when a legal entity consumes/combusts for the company's production, which contributes to the company's potential revenue, it is the consumption/combustion of the assets that contribute to this production that should be included. Emissions must therefore be measured for the assets included in the company's production and thus revenue, which means:

- consumption and emissions from the company's own assets which it uses for its own production, must be included
- consumption and emissions from leased assets used by the company for its own production, must be included.

The consequence of this logic is:

- consumption and emissions from an owned asset, which the company leases out to other companies' production, must not be included as scope 1, but the company that leases the asset must recognize it (see bullet 2).

However, if the company uses operational boundary logic, things are not that simple. A company that uses operational boundaries and that has employees to manage the operation of an asset is liable for the environmental impacts and safety incidents that arise from the activity of the asset – regardless of whether leasing in/out and who has the production. This means that if a company leases an asset with an operator, the lessee is not responsible for the emissions: it is the lessor. In other words, emissions from assets leased out to other companies' production with accompanying crew (ships, oil rigs, agricultural machinery, trucks, etc.) would need to have scope 1 data with the owner and thus the lessor, and not with the lessee and thus the user.

Consider the following: if a manufacturing company uses operational boundaries, it just has to make sure that all the equipment is leased with crew from outside, so that the company is not scope-1-responsible for anything: in other words, plenty of production, revenue, and cash flow, but no CO_2 emissions at all. Does that sound like the right solution?

A good counter-question from supporters of operational boundaries could be: is the lease income revenue or not? Yes, it certainly is. However, what does the company sell when leasing out an asset? It is not the activities of the asset, but access to involve the asset in the lessee's production for a limited period. Thus, the owning company sells a financing alternative to the lessee, who then does not have to buy the asset, and thus the lessor sells the lessee financial flexibility – that is it. Usually there are not many emissions from activities that ensure financial flexibility. This is also true even if the company leases the asset with crew. The argument for financial boundaries remains that the customer has chosen this asset and not another asset with some other features and with some other crew. Hence, the lessee itself determines:

•   the production that is to be carried out
•   where the production is to be carried out
•   the speed at which the production is to be carried out
•   and the means by which the production is to be carried out.

The lessee could have chosen not to produce or could have chosen a cheaper asset model that is more polluting and causes injury or death, or vice versa. If one believes that the lessee should be responsible for that choice, then one should choose financial boundaries.

The difficult distinction is between leasing with crew and sale of services. The difference is that a sale of services occurs when the vendor can decide which asset to perform the service with and thus include the decision on how much to pollute and how dangerous the work is. Thus, the customer of a service is therefore not scope-1-responsible – the service provider is. The service customer may also choose to include emissions data from this service, but it will be as scope 3 – if the company has chosen to work with scope 3, although that is currently not very widespread (see Chapter 5 "Proposed minimum data"). The IFRS has clear rules[12] for when the customer is leasing an asset with crew and when the customer is buying services. It is recommended that these rules be reused to ensure that there is 100 percent transparency on this point.

The above distinction about the allocation of emissions should be 100 percent parallel when working with safety data, whether the company selects financial or operational boundaries. However, if the company chooses financial boundaries, then it may be sensitive because employees with a contract with one company may have to be included in the safety statistics of another company that has leased the asset that the employee is operating. However, that is already the case today, since most of the standard safety rules from the authorities[13] state that people who are injured on a company's premises[14] (e.g. external consultants who fall down the stairs in the main office of their customer) must be reported by the customer to the authorities. It is the asset-using entity that is responsible for reporting to the authorities – regardless of employment. To ensure that we as a society do not double-count the dead and injured, it is vital that companies have decided who has the production of the asset with which (for example) a man came to be injured or killed. Then it is clear that it is this company that has to report on the accident.

Joint operations

In some industries, joint arrangements are widely used, whereby two or more companies join together for a production. From 2013, the IFRS has chosen to segregate joint ventures (JVs) and joint operations (JOs); the following section will only apply to JOs, as they are continuously to be line-by-line consolidated pro rata (see p. 41), while JVs are to be treated as associates and should therefore not be included in the consolidation. JOs therefore still impact on the revenue, production, and cash flow, while this is no longer the case for JVs. To understand the full distinction, see IFRS 11 (2012).

If the company is working with operational boundaries, then it will only include emissions, safety data, etc., from the JOs that it operates. One key question is therefore: how to become an operator? The answer is: it is unde-fined. It depends on who volunteers, who is in the area where the production is to take place, who has the equipment available or something else entirely random. Either way, the outcome of JOs is that the partner chosen as the operator will have to include 100 percent of the environmental and safety data, while the other JO partner has 0 percent in its reports – according to operational boundaries, that is.

The financial boundary situation is somewhat different: each JO partner will include its share of the production, revenue, cash flow, etc., regardless of operator distribution, and will therefore also include its share of emissions and safety data – if the company uses financial boundaries.

Consider this: financially, an oil company reports on large quantities of oil produced and a high revenue and cash flow, but in an operational boundary CSR report it has 0 in scope 1 emissions and 0 dead and injured, simply because it was smart enough to duck when the operator role was decided. Does this sound appropriate? It can certainly be mis-used, if some receive a bonus for the combination of EBIT[15] compared with CO_2, or EBIT in relation to safety data.

Fundamentally speaking, if a reporting relationship is to be established between the company's production data and its CSR data, then it must be a requirement that the JOs be incorporated on a similar pro rata basis, as they are financially. A good counter-question from supporters of the operational boundary data sets could be, why authorities are then satisfied with receiving only one operator report: have they not discovered this is inappropriate? Most likely they have, but for them it does not matter, and perhaps it is also a little troublesome to keep track of who owns what. When the authorities need data from a production unit, it is likely that they think that it is much easier just to speak to a single operator. Nevertheless, such arguments are of no importance to investor oriented CSR reporting, in which it is a requirement that there is full accordance between production data, revenue, CO_2 emissions, and the number of dead and injured.

Other generic problems with use of operational boundary data in CSR reports

In addition to the just-mentioned inconveniences associated with operational boundary data, there are also some more generic conditions that make these data very difficult to work with. First, the operational boundary is, as previously indicated, not a uniquely defined boundary scoping: it is given by industry standards and geographical norms and laws. The definitions and standards are different across industries and geography – and therefore a consolidated set of operational boundary data will be an addition of data that are not calculated in the same way. This kind of alternative data discipline would certainly not be accepted in financial contexts, in which the IFRS requires that all local financial accounts reverse the common IFRS rules before consolidation. In addition, in conglomerates, in which the companies in the corporation trade internally, there will be multiple instances of the same data, as various industry standards mean that the same data may be counted in more than one activity; thus, there are risks of double-counting. This is, of course, also a problem seen from an aerial view of society as a whole, as scope 1 GHG data in operational boundaries thus cannot be summed to give the total GHG emissions for the whole world: this would lead to massive double-counting.

Another problem is that the operational boundaries cannot be controlled for completeness. When the company and the auditor work with completeness in the financial universe, one is deftly delineated as what the company owns and controls (subsidiaries and JOs) and which assets the company owns and leases for its own use. This means that the company and the auditor can "simply" review the list of legal entities and assets and the production associated with these, thereby ensuring that everything is included: completeness is achieved. When working with operational boundaries, the whole world is in scope – including units and assets not owned or leased, which are contributing to others' production. Completeness has to be ensured through evidence from "outside the book": given that there are no external sources that can confirm what the company operates, it becomes impossible to ensure completeness.

Financial consolidation method

Further to the above, it is required that the consolidation method used throughout the CSR report is 100 percent parallel to the financial report. This means:

- subsidiaries incorporated 100 percent (regardless of minorities)
- JOs in proportion to ownership
- JVs and associates, etc., should not be incorporated.

This will also be in full compliance with the GHG Protocol's scoping definition, which requires that what the company controls, it must include data from – see IFRS 10 (2012) on definition of control.[16] It will ensure too that CSR data can be compared with all the lines in the financial report prior to deducting minority interests, such as revenue, EBITDA,[17] invested capital, cash flow, production volumes, etc. This in turn ensures that CSR data can have a context, whereby the investor can effectively assess whether the individual company performs well or poorly in relation to the environment, safety, social legislation, or whatever the investor wishes to measure. For example, CO_2 emissions can be compared with another measured factor in the company – for instance production volumes – and this information can also be compared with other companies in the same industry, just as it is possible with all sorts of other indicators in the financial report. Hence, the company is also better able to explain that even though it has potentially increased its production quantities, and the environmental impact of the company as a whole in absolute terms has grown, it may well be that the environmental impact per unit of production has decreased. The company does not have to incriminate itself just because it grows, as it may simultaneously perform better in relation to the environment per unit produced.

If the company chooses to use operational boundary data, it must – in addition to the previously mentioned disadvantages – also work with another case of inappropriateness in the consolidation, which is related to the rules and tools for consolidation of operational boundary data that have not been elucidated. If the company is working with financial boundary CSR data, then it has the great advantage of reusing the financial consolidation tool, and thus also reusing the benefits (IT audit, access restriction, audit trails, etc.) that are already built into the system. If the company must consolidate operationally, then the consolidation tree ("ownership tree") has to be made into an operational tree, which can also include legal entities that the corporation does not own and exclude entities that the corporation does own. In the financial universe, the company is working with "ownership-by-period", i.e. consolidation assuming given ownership and control per period (typically months) for the year. In contrast, when working with operational boundary data, the consolidation should work with "operation-by-period" since the decisive factor for the consolidation must take place on the basis of whether the company is the operator or not, which can change during the year. It is found, however, that there are no rules for this, and probably there are not many large corporations that can keep such a consolidation tree under control, not least because there are no external sources that can be used for reconciliation. This means that there are even more reasons to anticipate that there is no guarantee that the operational consolidation tree is complete, and therefore operational data cannot be reviewed for completeness.

Standard form for a minimum of CSR reporting

Just as there are now standard forms showing how an income statement, balance sheet, and cash flow should appear, there should also be a requirement for how CSR notes should be produced. This would allow data users to find and use data, as indicated by the Canadian Institute of Chartered Accountants: "The existence of a standard format or template for presenting information would assist investors in locating the data they want for decision making".[18] It would most certainly not be popular, for a number of CSR employees and especially communication agents, considering their sometimes very creative set-up of CSR reports (see Figure 4.1).

If the report is actually to be used for any purpose, then it is important that the investor does not have to scroll through thick reports or search in more or less structured online materials, or even sit and piece together the data that are needed. There are others who have found this to be true: the CSR rating or analytical agencies to which investors subscribe for information. If one considers what, for example, the major CSR rating or research agencies, like Bloomberg, SAM, or Thomson Reuters, require of CSR data, then the minimum form could be aptly divided as follows:

- environmental data
- social data
- governance data.

These are also called ESG data.[19] Which indicators, as a minimum, should be included for each of these areas is discussed in Chapter 5 "Proposed minimum data"; the standard presentation form for the note is given in Appendix G.

In addition to the indicator tables for the layout, the CSR report could be allowed the same segmentation as the financial report, as required by the IFRS.[20] This would also ensure that the CSR data across the corporation are comparable. Then, the reporting of CSR data would resemble the segment note in the financial report, which would be immediately recognizable to the investor and analyst. One could even consider letting the CSR minimum data be an extension of the required financial segment data in the financial report; more on this will be included in the next section on "Integrated reporting".

Integrated reporting

Today (before the IIRC framework – see p. 27), integrated reporting is a term that covers the integration of financial and non-financial reporting. At least two different definitions currently exist:[21]

- *The narrow meaning*: the financial and non-financial reporting are stapled into a single document without further interleaving, so that there are two sections: a financial and a non-financial section. This is also sometimes called a combined report.
- *The broader meaning*: here the financial and non-financial reporting are put together so that it is clear how the elements interact and affect each other's development.

Most companies will be able to implement integrated reporting in the narrow meaning without much work. However, for most CSR experts, this is not what they mean by integrated reporting. Rather, they would like to see

How shall the financial communnity take this seriously?

FIGURE 4.1 WestLB's appropriate question to Cadbury Schweppes' CSR Report[a] 2006, WestLB (2008)

a Based on an investigation made in 2007 by Garz, H., Volk, C. & Frank, K.

our business

At Cadbury Schweppes we manufacture, market and sell confectionery and beverage products. We are the world's largest confectionery company, and have strong regional beverage businesses in North America and Australia. With origins stretching back over 200 years, today our products are enjoyed in almost every country around the world.

Our strategic goals to deliver superior shareowner performance profitably and significantly increase global confectionary share; profitably secure and grow regional beverages share; ensure our capabilities are the best in class and nature the trust of colleagues and communities.

In 2005 we set financial goals to measure our annual business Performance based on these key performance indicators – sales margins and cash flow. For the 2004-2007 period we aim to grow revenues by 3-5% every year (excluding acquisitions and disposals) to improve margins by 50 to 75 basis points each year and to generate free cash flow of £15 billion.

We have made changes to our business portfolio to ensure that capital is applied where we can generate the highest growth and returns. We have further focused our beverages business on more advantaged markets though editing our beverage business in Europe, Syria and South Africa, and concentrating our beverage activities on the key markets of North America, Mexico and Australia, where we have strong brands and effective routes to market.

In beverages, we have strengthened our route to market in the US through a number of acquisitions. The most significant of these was the purchase, in the spring of 2005, of the 55% stake we did not already own in the largest independent bottler in the US, the Dr Pepper/Seven Up Bottling Group (which we renamed Cadbury Schweppes Bottling Group).

In confectionary, we intend to sell a number of non-core brands and businesses in the UK and Canada to allow us to focus on our more profitable and advantaged brand portfolio. We have invested over £100 million in emerging markets to increase our existing holdings in business in Nigeria and Turkey, and to acquiring the leading chewing gum business in South Africa.

Following the changes to our business described above, we will update our stakeholders on our strategy and plan for 2007 and beyond at the end of October 2006.

the broader sense used, as Novo Nordisk, Unilever, and SAB Miller have done for years, whereby the narrative part of the annual report is mixed together with elements from both the financial and the non-financial world. In fact, in South Africa, this has been common practice for listed companies since the Johannesburg Stock Exchange adopted the King III principles as part of its listing requirements in 2010; King III requires listed companies to apply its principles or explain which recommendations have not been applied and publicly provide reasons. King III recommends integrated reporting; hence the requirement for listed companies is to issue integrated reports. Since 2001, French listed companies have also reported in a framework of environmental, social, and governance indicators, and from 2012 this was enlarged to cover the large SME companies as well.[22] In the UK, it has also been mandatory from 2013 for listed companies to report on their GHG emissions as part of their annual Directors' Report.[23] Moreover, Denmark and Brazil have for some time had local regulations in this connection. See also UNEP *et al.* (2013) for a more detailed overview of local and regional rules and guidelines.

Integrated reporting in the broader sense will, however, continually have some formal requirements, as there are a number of formal requirements for the financial reporting tables and notes given in the financial regulations, i.e. the IFRS, which currently cannot be disregarded. Therefore, in these integrated reports there are still sections that only deal with financial figures – this is required for instance by the IFRS. Thus, as long as the IASB does not change this, the integration will only be in parts of the report. Hence, a completely integrated report in the broader sense cannot be achieved currently.

It has been difficult for many reasons to make these integrated reports common property among financial experts, not least because of problems with the reliability, relevance, comparability, and intelligibility for the primary financial annual report recipients: namely investors. Most of those interviewed for this book indicate that they believe that integrated reporting will become mandatory at some point for all listed companies in one form or another. "This is already coming…This trend will undoubtedly continue."[24] However, it is also indicated by many that it must make sense for the annual financial report users: "…as the accountancy profession still acknowledges that non-financial performance is relevant to overall company performance and the sustainability profession matures, together with policy makers 'Catching up' aspects of it will become mandatory."[25]

In the *Financial Times*, the CEO of the IIRC writes how he imagines that integrated reporting will influence investors' evaluation of the value of the shares:

it seems odd to analyse corporate governance in isolation from the way companies report to their investors and other stakeholders...The integrated reporting movement, which seeks to encourage companies to tell a clear, concise and comparable story about how they create and preserve value, is gaining momentum with businesses from more than 20 countries globally testing a new prototype integrated reporting framework, which seeks to help companies reveal hidden value, manage risks and contribute to more stable and efficient capital markets.[26]

Integrated reviews and the concept of materiality

One of the biggest problems with integrated reporting is integrating the audit/review of the two different information sets. Not least, the concept of materiality has a very different meaning for the two data sets. Financial materiality is defined in this way in accordance with ISA 320:[27]

- Fault information, including omissions, is considered material if it is reasonably expected that this information individually or combined would influence the economic decisions of users taken on the basis of financial statements.
- Evaluation of materiality is made under the given circumstances and influenced by the size or nature of the misstatement or a combination of the two.
- Evaluation regarding matters that are material to users is based on consideration of the general need for financial information as defined by users as a group. The potential impact of fault information on certain individual users, whose needs may vary widely, is not taken into account.

Non-financial materiality in the ISAE 3000 follows the above, because the ISAE 3000[28] has already defined which indicators are to be reported on, just as the indicators in the financial report are also predefined. This means that the auditor can simply assess whether the information provided, given these predefined indicators, is correct according to the materiality criteria that also apply financially. The big difference is, as mentioned in the section on the ISAE 3000 p. 23, that the statement may have two levels – a limited or a reasonable degree of assurance – with the result that the statement is either respectively negative or positive.

Different problems arise when we talk about non-financial materiality according to the AA1000, as this is a stakeholder-based process determined largely by the stakeholders. This means that the auditor's statement about materiality in an AA1000 context concerns the quality of the company's interaction with these stakeholders and the robustness of the process in the definition criteria for reporting, which is the result of this interaction. As shown, the materiality is something very different, depending on the regime within which the statement is made. Thus, it will be challenging to combine these concepts to form a whole in an integrated report that uses the AA1000 assurance for the non-financial indicators. Nevertheless, beyond the concept of materiality, there are also conceptual framework issues around the statement that should be considered. An audit statement should generally follow these demands:[29]

- *Intelligibility*: the information should be comprehensible to readers.
- *Relevance*: information is relevant if it makes a difference to the decision maker.
- *Reliability*: the information must be of a quality such that readers can rely on the content of the words being accurate, neutral, prudent, and complete.
- *Comparability*: readers should immediately be able to compare the content of the statements of other comparable companies, but also the statements of the same company year on year.

In particular, the requirements around intelligibility and comparability are problematic for non-financial statements, as financial readers will find it difficult to understand the very different statements, such as an ISAE 3000 statement with limited assurance, but even more so an AA1000 statement at any level, when compared with regular financial statements. As Sullivan (2011) explains it: "… as the approaches to the assurance of social and environmental performance have become increasingly technical, the language and presentation of assurance statements has become increasingly impenetrable to all but the specialists in the area (a group that excludes most institutional investors)."[30]

In an analysis of the statements made by auditors in general auditor firms (hereinafter referred to as auditors) and reviewers from environmental consultants (who are assumed only to have prepared AA1000 statements as they are not allowed to make an ISAE 3000 statement), Kamp-Roelands (2002) found the following differences:

- Auditors have a tendency to refer specifically to the pages of the report that is reviewed. Such specifications are rarely made by consultants.
- Auditors rarely give any explanation for their conclusion. Consultants offer many explanations and address many topics for the conclusion.

- Auditors provide only a brief (if any) description of the audit methodology. Consultants explain in detail their methods and practices, the improvements made by the company, and whether there are any outstanding recommendations from the review of the company involved.

Ceteris paribus, it will be very difficult for a non-CSR expert to understand a statement from a consultant. The statement is long, there is no fixed structure, and it contains criticisms or open recommendations that the company has not followed. Is that good or bad? The non-CSR expert will know nothing about the statement, and probably cannot come to his or her own conclusions about its content; the non-CSR expert may consider it very serious if the auditor felt compelled to give a critical statement. These are very rarely used in the financial world, in which such criticisms of conditions that are not material in financial terms are transferred to the protocol or the management letter, reserved for internal attention. It is not yet proposed in the IIRC integrated reporting framework to make an integrated statement, but if it were to be, consideration should probably also be given as to whether the AA1000 should be involved at all and whether it should be possible to harmonize the statement's form and content, to avoid scaring away the non-CSR expert. One can imagine the ISAE 3000 statement being broken down by the types of data[31] that are the same for all companies, and then concatenated with the classic financial statement. This statement must be made by IFAC members, partly because it both covers financial and non-financial data, partly because: "Investors will place more weight on the views expressed by one of the major accountancy firms than they will on views from stakeholder groups or corporate responsibility consultancies."[32]

Thus, if integrated reporting is to be more widespread and accepted, it will at least require an integrated auditor statement, and that will require a harmonization of the concept of materiality and recognition that data quality and reliability are at least equally as important as materiality.

CSR accounting principles

In the financial annual report, the investor can find descriptions of accounting principles; thus, the CSR report should also reflect how the CSR data have been defined and calculated.[33] The principles should include at least the following items:

- the principles for boundaries – operationally or financially; if operational boundary data are used, these principles must be specified further, because, as described earlier, industry and geography drive different definitions
- principles of consolidation
- the corporation's requirements for documentation of data locally – this may be divided by data type (see note 25)
- references for converters, as well as information on whether CO_2 data are measured or calculated
- specific definitions of specific data, if there are options
- information on the possible use of consumption standards.

We can therefore conclude that if we are to develop investor oriented CSR reports, they must be made with financial boundaries, they must be financially consolidated, and the data must be presented in strict forms that might be an extension of the already used financial segment notes. One can imagine the ISAE 3000 statement being broken down by the types of data that are the same for all companies. The data types should guide the kind of evidence that is needed for each indicator. If this is standardized, it will ensure that all CSR data are of comparable quality. If integrated reporting is used, an integrated auditor statement needs to be developed. Finally, it is vital that companies publish their CSR accounting principles, so that the investor and analyst can assess the data quality, as they would do financially.

Notes

1 In interview with François Passant, Executive Director, Eurosif. Slightly shortened.
2 ACCA & Eurosif (2013), p. 8.
3 FASB = Financial Accounting Standards Board (US-based)
4 Bernstein (2009), p. 9.
5 See Appendix D "XBRL".
6 Sullivan (2011), p. 17.
7 See Appendix C "Company overview".
8 CDSB (2012).
9 For some reason is it still legal in UK not to follow this requirement, but to still use operational boundaries or equity share boundaries – such data sets will therefore also be of no value to investors (see Defra (2013) p. 6.) If the CDSB (2012) framework, paragraph 2.20, is used by the company, which is also recommended by Defra, this unfortunate outcome is eliminated.

10 See for instance European Parliament and Council Regulation (EC) No. 166/2006 of 18 January 2006 (Article 5) and associated Instructions for the Implementation of the European PRTR (section 1.1.6).

11 In the financial world, the distinction between operational or financial leasing is pointless – in fact, most investors make artificial calculations on top of the financial reports to ensure the financial data on leasing are comparable – and therefore is also redundant non-financially. There is further discussion on IAS 17 and the new leasing proposal in IASB (2013).

12 See IFRIC 4 (2004).

13 See for instance Commission Regulation (EU) No. 141/2013 of 19 February 2013 implementing Regulation (EC) No. 1338/2008 of the European Parliament and of the Council on Community Statistics on Public Health and Health and Safety at Work, which describes how safety statistics should be reported to the EU authorities so that they can be included in the European Health Interview Survey (EHIS). Available online at http://eur-lex.europa.eu/LexUriServ/LexUriServ.do?uri=OJ:L:2013:047:0020:0048:EN:PDF

14 The company's premises can of course also be leased premises.

15 EBIT: Earnings Before Interest and Taxes.

16 According to IFRS 10, an operator will not have control, since the operator role does not mean increased exposure to variation of profits other than what the ownership allows for, and the operator can be removed/replaced by the owning parties. The operator is, in other words, simply an agent who has no control.

17 EBITDA: Earnings Before Interest, Taxes, Depreciation and Amortisation.

18 CICA (2010), p. 12.

19 The institutional investors (especially those signing on UNPRI – see Chapter 3 (p. 29) often have ESG departments, which deal with exactly this kind of investor information.

20 See IFRS 8 (2009) (Operating Segments). It is in fact also recommended by British legislation, see CDSB (2012).

21 Eccles & Krzus (2010).

22 Institut RSE Management (2012).

23 Defra (2013).

24 In an interview with Charles O'Malley, Head of Europe, AccountAbility.

25 In an interview with Dave Knight, Sustainability Services Director, TwoTomorrows.

26 Paul Druckmann (2012, November 18). Investors need a clearer picture of value creation. *Financial Times*.

27 Available online at www.ifac.org/sites/default/files/downloads/a018-2010-iaasb-handbook-isa-320.pdf

28 Iansen-Rogers & Oelschlaegel (2005).

29 Kamp-Roelands (2002).

30 Sullivan (2011), p. 118.
31 See Chapter 6 "Evidence requirements for valid and complete data".
32 Sullivan (2011), p. 117.
33 See also EFFAS and DFVA (2010) and Sullivan (2011).

5
PROPOSED MINIMUM DATA

In the previous chapters it was concluded that the investor wants quantitative comparable data of good quality. Therefore, a data set with minimum requirements will be defined in the following.

In 2005 it became mandatory for all listed companies in the EU to produce financial reports according to IFRS. It has been demonstrated several times that this legislation, which provides for the use of common financial accounting rules, has resulted in significantly better comparability across firms, countries, and industries. In addition, there are also generic signs that the quality of the reports has improved.[1] Moreover, it has also been demonstrated that the countries having mandatory CSR reporting, have in fact also improved their companies' sustainable development.[2] This knowledge should be used to the benefit of CSR reports and thereby the investor, and it is therefore proposed that a mandatory international accounting standard for CSR be established. Such international legislation could easily lean on UK law about mandatory reporting of GHGs for the listed companies in their financial reports, and especially the CDSB guideline for this, since it refers to the rules of IASB,[3] which ensure financial and non-financial data are comparable and provide context for each other. It is stated that investors and business leaders are the primary beneficiaries, comparability is paramount, and data boundaries must be defined financially – and there are many other good and useful parallels to the financial report. "Just as financial reporting standards have developed to support robust reporting, clear understanding, reliable decision-making and assurance activity, similar standards and minimum requirements are likely to evolve for CSR reporting."[4]

We could also take French legislation as an inspiration,[5] at least in so far as it has, since 2012, established requirements for reporting mandatory CSR indicators. However, more than half of these indicators are not quantitative; the requirement is often merely to report whether the company has policies for one thing or another, which is not particularly helpful for an investor to work with – it does not even indicate whether such policies are adhered to.[6] In addition, the French rules do not cover the boundaries of consolidation of data. The Sustainability Accounting Standards Board (SASB) – a CSR counterpart to the US FASB – are also working to develop standards. But they have chosen a solution in which they will develop standards per industry, which obviously is close to useless for conglomerates – and to some extent also for investors, who just want an overview of the performance of investment opportunities.

As concluded earlier, if investors are to be able to use CSR reporting for anything immediately, it is important to have defined a minimum data set that is measured and consolidated in the same way for all companies – regardless of industry, geography, or CSR maturity. Data still have to have the qualities described earlier, i.e. they must be:

- *Reliable*: the investor must believe in the veracity of the data.
- *Relevant*: the data must have an impact on investors' behaviour; what will lead the average investor to put money in, sell off, or hold on to the stock?
- *Comparable*: data must be comparable across companies, countries, industries, and time.
- *Understandable*: the data must be presented in a way that is understandable and usable to the investor.

In contrast to GRI, where the content principle of materiality is above all other principles, these quality principles are of equal standing. This means that if the data are relevant but not reliable, then they cannot be included. One would never financially include such data. Given that in their 2012/13 reports 22 percent of the 250 largest listed companies[7] in the world had to restate their CSR data back in time, and that in 74 percent of these cases this was due to updated calculation methods, simple errors, or scope change (not related to M&A[8] but simple boundary problems), then it must be concluded that the data quality is not yet good enough. The good news is that restatements of previous years are done in the first place – which is of course important from a comparability point of view – but it is also worrying that it has to be done so often.

In connection with this book, an analysis of the 50 largest listed companies in the world was carried out, to deduce which indicators they had chosen to report data for. The logic is that if more than half of these quite varied companies can report on a given indicator, then these indicators can be declared to be essential for all types of companies, and they are also obtainable for all kinds of companies. But before doing this research on the companies, ESG surveys from various rating agencies[9] were analyzed to figure out what indicators the investors want data for. Since the rating agencies sell this kind of information to investors, we must assume this comprises the data that the investors have requested. Thereby what was thought to be a gross list of possible indicators to report on was created. But it turns out that the companies also report on a plateful of indicators that the investors – or at least the rating agencies – do not ask for, for instance, number of employees divided by geographical area. Since it is not asked for by investors, this indicator will not be included in the minimum requirement proposal, even though 54 percent of the companies report on this indicator. An individual company can of course always report more than what is required as a minimum, because it is just that – a minimum.

The following will include the indicators that more than 50 percent of the companies report on and which are also sought by the ESG rating agencies. The result is a list of indicators that are deemed valid for all companies with FTEs, regardless of industry or geography, and which the investors are interested in. The list is broken down by the proposed standard form for CSR reporting,[10] which corresponds to the rating agencies' standard forms/surveys, which naturally are divided into Environmental, Social, and Governance data:

Environmental data are:

- CO_2 equivalents scope 1 (metric tonnes)
- CO_2 equivalents scope 2 (metric tonnes)
- energy (GJ)
- water consumption (m^3)
- waste by destination (metric tonnes)
- environmental data per quantities (i.e. CO_2e/production quantities[11]).

In the future consideration could also be given to including other air emissions (such as SO_x, NO_x, VOC) and loans and investments in environmental development, as these indicators were used by more than 40 percent of the companies – but for now they will be left outside the minimum requirements.

The following social data are all very much reported on and often sought by the rating agencies. In particular, the number of employees (FTEs) is often reported (86 percent of all 50 of the world's largest listed companies report on this – probably also because this is mandatory in many countries' statutory accounts). The number of FTEs will also be important when ensuring the data are complete (see Chapter 7 "How to create a good control environment") – thus, this data indicator is one of the most important.

Social data are:

- number of employees (FTE)
- employees by gender (FTE or percent)
- managers by gender (FTE or percent)
- Lost Time Injuries Frequency (LTIF) (LTIs/exposure hours)
- fatalities (number)
- training of employees (hours per employee)
- voluntary work for community (hours of work)
- donations (monetary unit).

As for environmental indicators, there are some social indicators that could have been part of the minimum required data set, for instance, employees per ethnic group or race, which is much used in the USA.[12] But the problem here is that in some countries, such as South Africa and Denmark, the gathering of such statistics would not be possible, simply because companies are not allowed to gather that kind of information about their employees (or customers, or anybody else for that matter). The indicator could be softened by using nationality instead of ethnicity/race – nevertheless, as "only" 46 percent of the companies report these data for their employees, for now it is left outside the minimum proposal.

The next topic is governance. If the same logic as for environment and social indicators was applied – that more than 50 percent of the companies should report on a given indicator for its inclusion – it would not be possible to define any minimum requirements, since the companies report very differently on this topic (some even just publish a picture of their board and leave it up to the reader to interpret what they want from that). But since the governance data are fairly easy to get hold of and since the companies do not have to gather data and consolidate from the entire organization to report on these indicators, it is suggested instead that the principles for good corporate governance for listed companies[13] established by many stock exchanges/authorities be used to guide what to include as minimum requirements.

Governance data are:

- size of the board (number of people)
- women on the board (number of people and percent)
- board meetings (number per year)

- average duration of service on the board (years)
- meetings of the audit committee (if there is one) (number)
- duration of the auditor's relationship with the company (years).

Given the recommendations for good governance, it can also be argued that there should be reports on the number of so-called "independent directors". In order to be independent, a director cannot:

- within the past five years have been a member of the Executive Board managerial staff of the relevant company, or an associate
- have received significant additional remuneration from the company/ corporation or an associated company in the capacity of a member of the Board of Directors
- represent a controlling shareholder interest
- in the past year have had a significant business relationship (i.e. personally or indirectly as a partner or employee, shareholder, customer, supplier, or member of management companies with similar connections) with the company or an associated company
- within the past three years have been an employee or partner of the external auditors
- be CEO of a company where there is a governing representative of the company
- have been a member of the Board of Directors of the company for more than 12 years
- have close family ties with people who are considered dependent.

The problem is that the term "independent" is not clear and can be interpreted in many ways; for example, what is a "significant remuneration"? When such a question is up for interpretation, it is close to useless for the investor, and will therefore not be included in minimum requirements, but it can, of course, be added as additional information if the company or the company's stakeholders find it valuable.

In the OECD guidelines for corporate governance[14] it is also stated that if there are large shareholders or shares with different voting rights (A and B shares), such information should be included in the corporate governance statement. Furthermore, it is stated that information about remuneration of the Board must be included. But since all of this is already included in most financial reports, it need not be repeated here. Even Berkshire Hathaway,[15] the only one among the 50 largest listed companies in the world to not provide a CSR report in any shape or form, already reports on these elements in its regular annual statement.

Given the above proposal for minimum ESG data, it is clear that two of the four points of the UNGC are not covered by these indicators: human rights and anti-corruption. The analysis of the 50 largest listed companies in the world and ESG rating agencies alike suggest that these two areas are not the first priority. There may be several reasons for this, but it is not necessarily an indication that investors and companies do not see the areas as important – more likely it is because it is quite difficult to obtain useful data for these areas. This book will not recommend inventing indicators that are difficult and/or expensive to get hold of, and that may not make sense for companies and/or investors, simply to meet non-judicial guidelines. But to the extent that companies find it important for them, they can attribute measurements for these areas beyond the minimum data.

But why is it better to have a standardized minimum set of indicators, rather than companies using the GRI or AA1000 principles, or other initiatives when selecting indicators? The ideas behind GRI, for instance, are really good - unfortunately, the solution is far below expectations, because while standardization is promoted, the framework gives total freedom to the companies to report on what they or their stakeholders want – two goals that are not immediately mutually compatible. This can be seen simply by reviewing some of GRI content and quality principles, which in themselves are contradictory:

- *Relevance and materiality*
  It is suggested that the company uses stakeholders to identify relevant and important indicators. Such a principle will produce data sets with no comparability either between companies or over time for each company, since the proposed stakeholder approach will result in companies using different stakeholders; even if they are the same, they can change interests over time and between companies. This means in fact that the use of this stakeholder approach, which takes precedence above all other principles, results in the exact opposite of the intention – it makes it impossible for the investor and analyst to make decisions based on this information, as data cannot be compared.

- *Intelligibility*
  The information must be comprehensible to users. This sounds fine, but it is so loosely defined that CSR reports have a tendency to be very long and creative in design, with many unimportant images included.[16]

Not least, there is almost always a new and exciting structure for each report and also over time for individual companies. Since there is no requirement for a presentation format, the communication of content to the investor is significantly more complicated than is strictly necessary. Furthermore, the content, as described in the section on integrated reporting (p. 43), is often not readily understandable by investors. In a class by itself are the review statements, which are often long, expressive of criticism, sometimes in a negative statement form, and thus not immediately comparable to financial statements. This does not help the content to be easily understood by the investor.

- *Reliability and verifiability*
  This idea is really good – any financial analyst must support this. However, firstly, it is currently not mandatory that the data are reviewed. Secondly, the CSR reports can be reviewed at different assurance levels. Thus, the company can choose a "limited" review, where the company does not have to prove quite as much as in the case of a more thorough review with a high/reasonable degree of assurance – in fact, the reviewer does not even have to do real substance auditing of the data. This means that the investor cannot confer the same degree of reliability to all reports, which is not conducive to comparability. In fact, looking at the 50 largest listed companies in the world, 90 percent have no or only limited review statements. This should probably be changed so that data validity and comparability are given highest priority; we will then be able to attribute to the CSR reports better future value for investors and analysts. One could consider whether to distinguish between review requirements, depending on the data types (see Chapter 6 "Evidence requirements for valid and complete data"), whereby the same data type is reviewed at the same level, meaning comparability is maintained.

- *Comparability*
  This principle sounds good – but, as mentioned, it is in contrast to the first and highest GRI content principle of materiality. Therefore, one will often notice that companies' CSR reports are not comparable over time or across companies.

In addition to the lack of comparability between companies and over time, one could also – with some justification – accuse some companies of reporting only on what they are good at: so-called cherry-picking. "It is therefore difficult to accept their reporting is a proxy for implementation, as it is easy for companies to report only on their achievements, and remain silent on their dilemmas or challenges."[17] If companies are required to report on a set of minimum data, then the opportunities for companies to cherry-pick are minimized – at least for the areas to which minimum data relate.

Having a set of minimum data does not necessarily mean that companies should not apply the stakeholder methodology, or that they may not show special company-specific data and thereby potentially reveal more about their specific company. Minimum data are just that – a minimum. The reporting can easily go well beyond the minimum data – but should never offer less. This ensures that there is both a basis for comparability across companies, industries, geographical areas, etc., and, at the same time, room for the individual company to show company- or industry-specific information which the company and/or stakeholders have identified as essential.

In the following, each indicator in the proposed minimum data set will be examined with more detailed definitions, instructions, and requirements for proof of data that companies should be able to use and demonstrate immediately.

All indicators are assumed to be collected within the financial boundaries and added using financial consolidation rules. With such a predefined set of indicators, with clearly defined boundaries and consolidation principles, and the definition that the primary beneficiaries of the indicators should be the investors, it will also be possible for auditors to conduct an ISAE 3000 examination with the same degree of assurance per data type, since the requirements for evidence are aligned.

Environmental data

Environmental data do not consist only of CO_2 data, but CO_2 is an important factor, since it is highest on many CSR agendas. When the company has collected and calculated the CO_2 data, it is not much extra work to also calculate the energy use. This is important, as it can show how energy efficient the company is. In addition to CO_2 and energy, if the company has employees, it will surely also consume water and produce waste – this logic works for all companies all over the world. And finally, the company must also ensure the context of these environmental elements and compare them with the quantities produced (or another denominator), so that it is possible to assess how well the company is performing environmentally compared to its competitors, but also compared to itself over time.

When reporting on "CO_2", usually what is meant in reality is CO_2 equivalents which is an umbrella term for GHGs, consisting of a large number of gases such as CO_2, CH_4, and N_2O. They all have a different Global Warming Potential (GWP), a term that takes into account the wavelengths at which each gas absorbs radiation and its atmospheric residence time. These different gas emissions must therefore be recalculated to the standard unit called the "CO_2 equivalent" (CO_2e) which can then be consolidated in order to get an aggregate measure of the GHGs that are emitted – for example:[18]

* carbon dioxide (CO_2) – 1 ×
* methane (CH_4) – 25 ×
* nitrous oxide (N_2O) – 298 ×
* sulphur hexafluoride (SF_6) – 22,800 ×
* hydrofluorocarbons (HFCs) – depends on the type
* perfluorcarbons (PFCs) – depends on the type.

The six GHGs are the so-called Kyoto gases, named after the Kyoto agreement on minimizing their discharges. The CO_2 equivalents are, as described in the section on the GHG Protocol (p. 17), divided into scopes 1, 2, and 3. The minimum data only include scopes 1 and 2.

CO_2 equivalents scope 1 (metric tonnes)

If an entity measures GHGs directly from its emissions, the company should use these measurements as they are deemed to be the most accurate. In addition, the company can then also directly measure if there is any environmental benefit from any filters and other devices which it may have installed and which should reduce the amount of GHG emissions. But actually, it is rare for a company to measure their GHG emissions specifically. Most often it will be necessary to collect quantitative data on combusted fuels/materials and multiply these quantities by standards also known as converters for emissions of GHGs. There are therefore two components to the calculation of CO_2 that are important:

* choice of converters
* the definition of scope 1.

When selecting converters, the company must be aware that there is a myriad of these sets of converters[19] and should therefore choose these in accordance with some standard rules, whereby there is some consistency in the choice:

- Internationally recognized generic converter sets are preferred to ensure comparability across companies.
- Latest converters are preferred.
- A primary set of converters must be chosen and used in full. This means that a company cannot combine the sets, unless specific, additionally needed converters are not part of the primary set. This rule also prevents cherry-picking of converters.
- Specific industry converters may be used, if these are not in conflict with the above. This rule is subordinate to the other three.

The name(s) of the primary set(s) of converters must be published as part of CSR accounting policies, as it is an important detail in line with providing information about depreciation rates in the financial report. The company will typically gather CO_2 sources in uniform fuel groups with similar units – this is typically metric tonnes (as most converters refer to metric tonnes), but can also be in other units, e.g. litres or kWh. These groups might be:

- oil
- gas
- diesel
- gasoline
- kerosene
- coal
- biomass.

These groups should furthermore be subdivided, for example, into types of oil or coal, whereby it will be possible to use the converter set selected in accordance with the above principles. Here, it is important to get tested up front, potentially by asking local reporting entities, what types of fuels the companies' assets are using so that the corporate reporting can be as precise as possible. If the local entities are measuring fuel with different units, it is also important that the corporation makes conversion tables available to local entities. Thus, the consolidation of data should only take place on the basis of one measurement unit.[20]

One of the positive outcomes of measuring CO_2 via the consumption of fuels is that it is extremely rare for the company not to pay for these. Therefore, it is possible to document the consumption rather accurately using creditors' invoices that the company can find and document, via its bookkeeping, and the validity and completeness principles used in the financial audit.

Accruals from the financial accounts must be reused when producing CSR data, so that fuel received but not yet billed by the vendor must be included using the delivery notes – and vice versa for non-received but invoiced fuels. Those who work with stocks of fuels must also reuse the usual accounting from these, so that the company uses the calculated consumption (opening stock + purchased fuel during the period – closing stock).

For those who share offices and/or facilities, where fuel use is also shared, the regular local allocation key for costs should also be applied to fuel consumption. Some landlords of offices are not willing to provide information about the consumption of fuels for heating, but forward a fixed invoice which covers rent, electricity, heat, etc., all within one total figure. In these cases – and only in these cases, not because it is easier, and only for offices, since they are roughly comparable in consumption – the company can consider developing office standards,[21] which may be based on FTEs, area (m²) or something equivalent per geographical area. This ensures that headquarters can control for completeness, since all legal entities in the corporation can and have to report. More about this can be found in Chapter 7 "How to create a good control environment".

From the analysis of the 50 largest listed companies in the world, it appears that an array of these (36 percent) also measure CO_2 emissions from air travel – most likely done by measuring the number of airmiles and multiplying them by converters. A company should be aware that unless it uses its own/leased airplane or helicopter, air travel falls under scope 3 emissions: the company just receives a service for its employees to be flown from A to B.[22] Scope 3 emissions should not be included in scope 1, but may be reported on their own as scope 3; such reporting would provide extra data beyond the minimum but the company may think it is important. The same distinction should be used when working with transport of goods – see also the previous discussion about leasing and sale of services in Chapter 4 "Rules that ought to exist".

CO_2 equivalents scope 2 (metric tonnes)

Scope 2 CO_2 equivalents are related to the purchase of electricity and district heating produced by a third party but used by the company. The collection and validation of data on electricity and district heating work as for direct consumption of fuels, namely through booked invoices and delivery notes. The big difference is that geographical fragmentation of these data must be involved: there are very large differences in the emission of CO_2 equivalents from, for example, Iceland, Poland, and China, as the fuel basis for electricity and district heating in individual countries is very different.

If the company is producing the electricity or district heating itself, then typically these will be defined as scope-1-related (see previous section, p. 17). If surplus heat from production is used to heat up the buildings, then that is already taken into account in scope 1 and must not be added again in the emission calculation. If the company is buying renewable energy (wind, solar, geothermal, etc.), then there are in principle no emissions from these sources.

Energy (GJ)

Different fuels vary in their energy efficiency as measured by the amount of CO_2 equivalents they emit compared with the energy they produce. That is why, in addition to CO_2 equivalents, companies also report on energy consumed. Energy is typically calculated based on converters on fuel consumption and purchased electricity and district heating but, as for GHGs, the company can also measure the consumed energy directly.

Once the company has a total figure for the consumed energy, it is then possible to relativize this with the total scope 1 and 2 CO_2 equivalents, whereby one can see how energy efficient the company is. The consumed energy must be added from both scope 1 and scope 2, but must additionally contain energy figures from consumption of renewable energies. Thus, the more renewable energy used, the better the energy efficiency, as there are no emissions from renewable energy.

Water consumption (m³)

All companies employing people will also consume water. Since water is a limited resource, there are many companies that report this consumption (68 percent of the 50 largest listed companies in the world) – just as most research agencies also collect this information, so that investors can assess water use in relation to production. Water consumption should be "scoped" as the company scopes reporting of CO_2 – i.e. requiring only direct "scope 1" water consumption, according to the rules for financial boundaries and consolidation. If the company wishes to involve water consumption from "scope 3", it may choose to do so – but it should be clear in the report that these are extra data beyond the minimum and must be reported separately, so that the investor can decide to include or exclude these data as needed.

Water consumption is a little different from fuel combustion from the point of view of documentation, as it is not always something that the company must pay for – especially in developing and newly industrialized countries – and therefore there are not always invoices and delivery notes to document the consumption. The company must use invoices and delivery notes as far as possible, as they are the best form of documentation – but in areas where the company does not have that option, it can measure consumption itself or use the methods described in Chapter 6 under the section on probable data (see p. 80), i.e. estimating consumption on the basis of standard consumption elsewhere.

Water consumption can be split into sources, as this indicates more about the quality of water consumed – but this is beyond what is required in the minimum data, and is currently only done by 26 percent of the 50 largest listed companies in the world. Source types can be:

- drinking water
- groundwater (not approved for drinking water)
- surface water
- seawater
- collected rainwater.

Sometimes the company may not know which type of source is involved. In these cases the company must assume the "worst case scenario", which is the use of drinking water.

A frequently asked question is: can the company deduct cleaned water from the company's water consumption? If the company can prove the quantities and can prove that the water quality after cleaning is just as good as (or better than) when it tapped and then treated/purified the water, and that discharged water does not cause problems, then the company may deduct these amounts from their water consumption. But the company should report the water consumption in gross figures, whereby the investor can decide whether there can be deduction for treated/purified water in the analysis.

Waste by destination (metric tonnes)

If the company employs people, then there is certainly waste. Waste has the same documentation restrictions as water, since it is far from always the case that the company has documentation in place, as it may not have to pay to get rid of its waste. In most northern European countries, companies must both perform sorted garbage collection and pay to get rid of the sorted waste, whereby they have really good and solid evidence for their waste. But it is not necessarily so for all companies on the planet – in these cases, the entity shall apply the methods described in Chapter 6 in the section on probable data, (p. 80), i.e. estimating waste production on the basis of standards from elsewhere.

Waste must be broken down by destination (62 percent of the 50 largest listed companies in the world are able to do this), which can be:

- recycling (composting and reuse)
- combustion
- landfill
- special treatment (hazardous waste[23]).

If in doubt about the waste destination, the company should choose landfill as the "worst case scenario". Some also choose to report their waste given the type of waste (paper, plastic, metal, electronic equipment, etc.) – but this is fairly rare (only done in 16 percent of the 50 world's largest listed companies' reports) and is therefore not part of the minimum data set.

Environmental data per quantities

When all environmental figures have been compiled, it is time to relate the data to the company's production quantities in the period. This ensures that environmental data can actually be used for something when the investor evaluates performance relative to the company's competitors and the company's own history.

It is important to remember that it is not only manufacturing and mining companies who can measure quantities of their outputs. This is also the case for companies in the tertiary sectors who, in order to measure and report on how much they have produced, perhaps will have to be a bit more inventive. A service company must therefore make clear which unit drives the consumption of fuel and water and produces waste. It may, for example, be the number of services, such as a hairdressing chain that measures the number of customer transactions, or a haulier who measures the number of kilometres driven, number of loads, or a combination thereof. But it could also be a bank, for example, that can measure the number of employees or area (m²) of branches and offices.

The vast majority of industries already have some industry standards for how companies should measure quantities. The only thing which unfortunately sometimes goes wrong in terms of these industry standards is the rules for consolidation, which do not always follow the financial rules or may not have been correctly or clearly defined. It is still very important that the volumes are calculated according to the traditional financial scope and consolidation rules, whereby the data can give the context that ensures the newly calculated environmental figures, revenues, cash flow, etc., are comparable. The relative data included in the minimum data are:

- (scope 1+2 CO_2e)/quantities
- energy/quantities
- total water consumption/quantities
- total waste generation/quantities.

See Chapter 8 "How can investors use CSR in their analysis of stocks?" for more inspiration on ratios.

Social data

Social data are intended to inform the investor about how many employees are required to produce the newly determined quantities, how staff and management are composed, how much training the employees receive, whether employees have a risk of injury or death in the company's production methods, and what social commitments the company makes with its externalities in the form of contributions, donations, etc. A side effect of gathering social data for a well-performing company is that it can signal these data to present and future employees and thereby possibly retain and attract future necessary talent, who may see such matters as a priority. Social data can therefore also be seen as important in engendering the investor's trust in the company's continued growth.

Full-Time Equivalents (FTEs) – total, by gender and management layers

Social indicators concerned with the number of employees are already a requirement in many statutory financial reports and statistical reports to the authorities, but often these indicators are not precisely defined (e.g. "indicate the average number of employees").[24] It sounds very simple, but it is not. For instance, consider how differently FTEs are calculated in an OECD report[25] from 2013 – and this is still oversimplified, as can be seen in Table 5.1.

Some – especially HR employees – are mostly concerned about the number of heads, also referred to as the headcount (HC). This is understandable given

TABLE 5.1 Differences in OECD FTE reporting methodologies

Country	Method used for Full Time Equivalent (FTE) calculation
Australia	An FTE employee is calculated as working at least 70 hours over a two-week period
Czech Republic	40 hours per week used as an FTE
Estonia	The normal working time is 40 hours a week
Germany	The number of FTEs is calculated by adding the full- and appropriate proportion of part-time occupied employees on the basis of the standard working time (i.e. contractual working time of a full-time employee)
Israel	40 hours per week used as an FTE
Japan	FTE is calculated as (the staff's working hours for one week)/(the regular working hours for one week set by the establishment); in a case where the person works only a few days in a month, the calculation is (the staff's working hours for one month)/((the regular working hours for one week set by the establishment)×4)
Korea	40 hours a week
Norway	FTE data are calculated as contracted man-hours divided by full-time working hours in the reference week; all working contracts in the range of 32–40 hours are defined as full-time in order to account for shift workers
Slovak Republic	Normal working time is 8.5 hours per day
Switzerland	Original data collected in the surveys for nursing homes and community nursing organizations
United States	Usual hours worked per week for the past 12 months; if greater than or equal to 40 hours, then the individual is considered to be working full-time

the job they have, in which they must ensure each employee's progress in the company. But for companies with large seasonal fluctuations, many hourly workers, employees with a lot of compensated overtime, or employees on reduced hours, HC will be a particularly bad indicator of the company's workforce as a whole – even if calculated as an average. The reason is that the company cannot compare these kinds of data across companies, nor within the company itself over time – data cannot be related to production or staff costs since these data sets are not comparable. Thus, HC is not a good indicator in a CSR report.

As an example, if Danish Supermarket Group compute their number of employees as HC on 31 December, they would have about 40,000 employees due to the seasonality of Christmas and New Year trading and the upcoming January sales. But if they measure staff numbers by FTEs, then there would only be approximately 25,000 full-time jobs. Thus, there can be a significant difference.[26]

In addition, HCs frequently suffer all of the classic problems that come with boundaries and consolidation of data, which are also present for environmental data. Often, various HR systems are not set up to consolidate data correctly if the company has joint operations and/or cross-ownerships, etc. Furthermore, some HR systems also use operational scoping, so with joint operations, where the company is not the operator, the HR system has no data from these parts of the company's production. These kinds of data do not reconcile with staff costs, which makes the FTE data non-contextual and means their value is very limited. Therefore, and also because the number of employees may be driving the office standards discussed in the section on environmental data (p. 63), it is very important that the company and its auditors are very careful about getting the right evidence for the employee data that are to be included in their official reports. Companies will be best served by consolidating data from local payroll offices through regular financial consolidation of the FTEs – potentially together with consolidation of staff costs, whereby it is easier to detect incorrect reporting.

FTEs should be based on the actual number of salary/wage compensated hours a year compared to standard hours for a full-time employee; standard hours are very different around the world, so the company must calculate this figure locally. This allows the FTEs to be documented strongly through the payroll offices' generic salary/wage reconciliations. Even for employees in salaried positions, who just get a monthly salary without overtime compensation, it can be determined how many days there are in a norm year and how long the individual person has been employed. So good sources of evidence are certainly present and should be used.

When the company is setting the boundaries for who should be involved in the calculation of number of FTEs, it has to constantly keep in mind that the FTE figure must be held comparable with the staff costs. This means that when a company calculates the number of employees, it cannot include temporary workers paid by invoice to an agency or the like. The company must not involve employees on unpaid leave, as there is no compensation given in this case, whereas employees on paid leave must be involved.

Given the segment reporting[27] suggested in Chapter 4 "Rules that ought to exist", it is also important that the company is able to calculate the employee distribution per segment properly. A recurring and valid question is: how should employees be split who are "borrowed" from one part of the company by other parts of the company, or a receptionist whom two companies/segments share at a given address? If it is a split within a legal entity but across business units, then the legal entity will generally be able to make a simple FTE split in accordance with the staff cost split. If the "loan" is across legal entities, what must be considered is whether this is a sale of services or "pass-through" of the cost of the employee (with a fixed mark-up in respect of transfer pricing regulations). If it is a pass-through, then the FTE should be added to the legal entity that uses the employee – it must therefore be regarded as a "lease" of the individual employee. In contrast, if the case is sale of services, then there is no question that the service recipient should not include this employee in their FTEs (fully or partially). The receiver has received a service and the employee is to be included in the FTE statistics from the area in which the employee gets his salary.

Regarding the split of FTE numbers by gender and management layers, the company can benefit greatly by simply asking for a total note of the number of employees per management layer by gender – and thereby in one go, through the regular financial consolidation rules, also find the total number of FTEs for the company as well as the gender split. This will also ensure that there is always a reconciliation between the financial note on the number of employees in the staff cost note and the CSR reporting.

The tricky aspect of this splitting of the data is to define when a person is a manager. Are a certain number of subordinates required to be a manager, or can an employee be a manager without staff responsibility (e.g. highly influential specialists)? Is it a matter of whom the individual reports to, or whether the individual has a direct impact on other employees' daily work without necessarily having to do staff appraisal (i.e. by being the person who defines rules and regulations which other employees must observe)? There are no clear answers to all these questions, but Table 5.2 includes a split that

TABLE 5.2 When is an employee a leader?

Name of management layer	Description
Corporate Presidents and Vice Presidents	Corporate and business unit senior management
Directors	• Leaders of managers • Specialists with direct impact on decisions made by President and Vice President level • Specialists with direct impact on managers' daily work
Managers	• Functional managers • Leaders of other employees • Specialists with direct impact on decisions made by directors • Specialists with direct impact on other employees' daily work
Other employees	Everyone else

most companies can use. When all four layers are added, the company can find the total number of FTEs.

Lost Time Injuries Frequency (LTIF) (LTIs/exposure hours)

Accidents are one of the earliest matters that companies have been required to report to the authorities. Local authorities have their own rules on how this should be done and how to decide when there has been an accident within the definition of "Lost Time Injuries" (LTIs). In some countries the requirement is that the employee should have been away from his or her job for at least 72 hours before the accident is to be included in the statistics; in others, the requirement is 24 hours. There are also different criteria that are used to define when a company is responsible for reporting the accident. Thus, to consolidate the data for corporate reporting, it must be required that all reporting entities use the same definitions and put aside what they have reported to various local authorities. That is the only way to gain a reasonable data set that does not consist of "apples and oranges".

An accident must be work-related, and should result in the victim being unable to work for at least 24 hours after the day of the accident. The accident is work-related when the accident occurs on or by the company assets pursuant to financial boundaries (see Chapter 4, "Rules that ought to exist") and is an outcome of the work environment. An accident involving more than one person should be counted as the number of people affected by the accident and not one accident per se. Accidents can involve a company's own employees, contract workers, subcontractors, and third parties, and should be divided into these categories. Accidents also include fatalities.

To put the LTI number into perspective, the company should also count the number of hours during which accidents may occur, called "exposure hours". In order for the data to be comparable, it is important to collect exposure hours data for the company's own employees, contracted staff, and subcontracted staff. For good reasons, it is quite impossible to collect data on exposure hours for third parties; in most cases it is also very difficult to gather data on subcontractors.

The numbers must include all working hours including overtime and training on company premises, but not periods of sickness and leave. The figures also do not include the time in which the employee acted as another company's "asset" (e.g. time when the employee was leased out along with an asset). In these cases, the lessee is responsible for collecting exposure hours and LTI data.

In cases where the company does not have accurate timing, then the FTE calculation basis can be reused. It is inaccurate – the employees can be compensated for hours not exposed to accidents at or by the companies' premises and vice versa and therefore it implies risks of both over- and understatements of exposure hours – but it may be the best-documented data set the company has. In the case of contracted staff, the company can sometimes assume from their contracts how many hours they have been at or by the company's premises – at other times, unfortunately, a qualified estimate must be used.

Now the company can calculate the LTI frequency, broken down as the LTIs on its own employees and contract workers – and possibly subcontracted workers, if the break-down can be supported by the exposure-hour data. The formula is given under "Lost Time Injuries frequency" in Appendix F. It is important to note that some authorities demand the LTI frequency to be calculated based on 200,000 exposure hours and others on 1,000,000; this will of course make a huge difference to the frequency and, therefore should this calculation also be standardized? It is suggested that it should be against 1,000,000 exposure hours, as this is what is most widely used. It is important to collect the LTIs and exposure hours separately, whereby it can be assured that controlling and consolidation at headquarters can be done correctly and a consolidated frequency can be calculated.

Fatalities (numbers)

A fatality is work-related when an accident happens on or by the company's premises pursuant to financial boundaries, and is an outcome of the work environment. These fatalities can involve the company's own employees, contracted workers, subcontractors, and third parties, and should be divided into these categories. Fatalities do not include suicides or other fatalities which are non-work-related.

Given the financial boundaries, the company should not include fatalities where the company's own employees were killed at another company's assets (e.g. if the employee was leased out along with an asset). In these cases the lessee is responsible for reporting on the fatality. The company should probably explain the fatality in its report, but should ensure this incident does not impact the statistics. The same goes for fatalities that occur in a joint operation. In these cases the proportional fatality[28] in the statistics should be explained in the text.

This way of working with the health and safety data will also ensure that conglomerates with many intercompany trades can provide valid health and safety data for the corporation with no double counting, which would otherwise be impossible. And from an aerial perspective, it is also better for society or industry that it is possible to consolidate to a higher level without double counting fatalities.

Training of employees (hours per employee)

Training consists of a variety of activities internally as well as externally. The external part is fairly easy to document, as the company usually pays for this; therefore the number of hours can be found via invoices for training. It is of no importance whether the training hours are within working hours or not, as long as the training is paid for by the company. It is likewise not important whether there is an exam at the end of the training for it to qualify as training. But conferences and meetings in experience fora, etc., are not considered as part of training.

The more tricky part is assessing the quantity of internal training. Often companies will have Learning Management Systems (LMS), and these can provide good documentation of how many hours employees have spent on the online training made available to them. Additionally, if the company has formalized internal training courses face-to-face, it is somewhat easy to track how many hours multiplied by the number of employees that have attended, though it is impossible to produce evidence of completeness. Likewise is it impossible to document the hours of peer-to-peer training. Internal training hours need to be established bearing in mind these limitations. Therefore, training hours must be split between external and internal hours; this practice would also take into account the fact that demands for documentation and the level of assurance are different.

The number of employees included in the denominator is of course based on the FTEs calculated earlier and not based on headcount.

Voluntary work for community (hours of work)

This indicator is much used by the 50 largest listed companies in the world: it is reported on by 62 percent of them and it seems to be an especially popular indicator for companies with headquarters in North America and Asia. But at the same time, ensuring its validity is very problematic – thus it is with some hesitation that it is included in the minimum required data.

To be able to qualify as voluntary work by the company, the hours worked have to be a donation by the company and not by the employees – thus, they must be hours of work that are contributed to local community/ies within working hours; whatever good deeds the employees are doing outside of working hours cannot be included.

It may be possible to recognize these hours while doing the exposure-hour calculation for the LTIF, as most work of this kind is not done on company premises. This could be one way of providing indirect proof. Another form of proof may be provided by the individual employee writing a diary about when, and how much, voluntary work is taking place and potentially also explaining what is being done; this information could be added to the text, describing in what way the voluntary work contributes to local communities. For example, it may have to be explained why the work performed is a contribution and not a burden or of no importance to the recipient local community.

Since this kind of indicator is less likely to be underestimated, the primary test direction must be validity. The company must be able to prove the hours included are valid and that the tasks achieved are of benefit. If no such proof exists, no hours can be included.

Donations (monetary unit)

By far the most used CSR indicator is that of donations; 90 percent of the 50 largest listed companies in the world report on this indicator. However, there are problems with it: the most significant lie with distinguishing between advertising and donations – this is where CSR should not be an extended arm of the PR department. The distinction must be made by looking at the purpose of the donation: if the donation is aimed at selling/promoting the company's products or name, then these "donations" are simply advertising and should not be included as donations. If the company wants to tell and show pictures of their promotional activities, then it must be considered as additional information, which the company of course can include in the CSR report – it should just be clarified that it is not part of the minimum data that make up the donations indicator.

Information on donations must be given without the company having or wanting to have any advertising effect; it may even be that the company does not want the donation to be known. It is exactly these non-visible donations that should be involved. Donations need to be comparable, and grouped as follows:

- benevolent purposes
- political parties
- other associations
- anonymous grants for activities or acquisitions.

Some companies are wholly or partly owned by foundations. These foundations are separate legal entities, and as such are not involved in the company's CSR reporting. The foundation can choose to establish its own CSR report on donations, contributions, etc.

Governance data

Governance data are often described in the annual statement of corporate governance, which many stock exchanges/authorities demand the listed companies provide. This data set is relatively simple to obtain and validate – in this CSR context the purpose is mainly to make these data readily available to the investor, since the corporate governance statements are often placed separately to other reporting, they are often long and difficult to read, and, unfortunately, they also have a tendency to be generic from one year to the next. In some cases, there may also be a need for greater precision than is the case in the current corporate governance statements; for example, while in the statements it is acceptable to describe "two to three meetings", what will be required in this reporting will be to verify whether there were "two *or* three meetings" in the year.

Size of the board (number of people)

Size is measured by number of people. If the board has changed size over the reporting period, the number at the end of the period is to be reported. The size is calculated both including and excluding potential employee representatives.

Women on the board (number of people plus percent)

The number of women on the board is measured in number of people. If the board constellation has changed over the period, the number of women at the end of the period is to be reported. The number of women is calculated both including and excluding employee representatives.

Board meetings (number)

This is the number of board meetings held during the period calculated pursuant to board meeting minutes.

Average duration of service on the board (years)

The average duration on the board is calculated in years at the end of the period. Seniority is the total number of years each member has been a member, even if there have been one or more breaks in membership. This duration is added up per member and divided by the size of the board identified previously. Seniority is determined both inclusive and exclusive of employee representatives.

Meetings of the audit committee (if there is one) (number)

If the company has an audit committee, it must be determined how many meetings have been held during the reporting period pursuant to audit committee meeting minutes. If there is no audit committee, this is indicated by a dash or n/a, not with 0, since that would indicate that the audit committee does exist but has not met.

Duration of the auditor's relationship with the company (years)

Seniority of the current auditor relationship is calculated in years at the end of the reporting period. If there are two auditors, then two durations must be reported. The seniority of the auditor relationship is linked to the signatory auditor personally and not to the auditor firm. Seniority is determined by the total number of years the auditor has been signatory auditor of the company, even if there have been one or more pauses in the relationship. The duration should be reported for both the financial auditor and non-financial auditor/reviewer.

Notes

1 Yip & Young (2012).
2 Ioannou & Serafeim (2012).
3 CDSB (2012).
4 Interview with Lois Guthrie, Executive Director, CDSB, and former Technical Director of the IIRC.
5 Institut RSE Management (2012).
6 Morris (2012).
7 KPMG (2013).
8 M&A = Mergers & Acquisitions
9 Bloomberg, SAM, Corporate Nights, FTSE4GOOD, Thomson Reuter's ASSET4, and KLD.
10 See also Appendix G on suggestions for CSR note forms.
11 CO_2e = CO_2 equivalents
12 See for instance Walmart's CSR report (p. 84): http://corporate.walmart.com/microsites/global-responsibility-report-2013/pdf/Walmart_GRR.pdf

13 For example: http://www.frc.org.uk/Our-Work/Codes-Standards/Corporate-governance/UK-Corporate-Governance-Code.aspx, http://www.nasdaqomx.com/digitalAssets/85/85404_cgnordicproject2011.pdf

14 OECD (2004).

15 http://www.berkshirehathaway.com/2012ar/2012ar.pdf

16 See for instance WestLB (2008).

17 Hamid & Johner (2010), pp. 269–270.

18 See for instance: http://www.ipcc.ch/publications_and_data/ar4/wg1/en/ch2s2-10-2.html; http://www.climatechangeconnection.org/emissions/documents/GWP_AR4.pdf

19 See for instance Intergovernmental Panel on Climate Change (IPCC), International Energy Agency (IEA), Department for Environment, Food & Rural Affairs (UK) (Defra), United States Environmental Protection Agency (USA) (EPA), etc., who all publish different sets of converters that can be applied internationally.

20 See also Appendix E for conversion tables.

21 International office standards ought to be developed, as this is a widespread problem. Until these are developed, and if a company does not have any standards or the opportunity to develop some based on historical reports, it should consider contacting other companies who may be willing to share their standards.

22 See also the section "Greenhouse Gas Protocol Initiative" on p. 18 in Chapter 3 "Rules and guidelines that exist" and the section "Leasing" on p. 36 in Chapter 4 "Rules that ought to exist" to gain a deeper explanation of GHG scoping and sale of services.

23 Examples of hazardous waste include: oil, paint, solvents, poisons, fertilizers, acids, chlorinated waste, mercury-containing waste, batteries, aerosols, gunpowder.

24 See for instance: http://www.hmrc.gov.uk/manuals/vcmmanual/VCM13120.htm or http://epp.eurostat.ec.europa.eu/statistics_explained/index.php/Glossary:Full-time_equivalent

25 OECD (2013).

26 2012 figures.

27 IFRS 8 (2009).

28 Proportional fatality can occur in a report for a corporation, if the fatality happens in a joint operation, since joint operations are pro rata consolidated per line item given the ownership percentage. The other partner(s) in the joint operation will likewise report their proportion of the fatality, the outcome being that for society there is one fatality from this incident. See also the section "Financial consolidation method" (p. 41) in Chapter 4 "Rules that ought to exist".

6

EVIDENCE REQUIREMENTS FOR VALID AND COMPLETE DATA

In the previous section, each indicator in the minimum data set was defined in detail. This section addresses the evidence the company must obtain for each indicator and the means by which the evidence can be declared valid and complete, depending on the data type.

Many believe that CSR reporting is much harder to validate and review compared to financial reporting. Many believe that there is a much larger element of "guesswork" or estimation than there is in financial reports. But it does not have to be this way. Most accountants are well aware that a financial report is not an expression of a higher truth: it is "only" the best attempt at a fair presentation. Think of the evidence for provisions, contingent liabilities, or intangible assets. These items are not an expression of ultimate truth, but they are the best attempts at one. In contrast, it is relatively easy to undertake bank reconciliation as it draws on strong evidence; the company can use its bank statements and the auditor can also refer to engagement letters.[1] Just as a financial report consists of both items that can be verified fairly easily and more complicated items, so it is with a CSR report.

Requirements for documentation

As described in the section on ISAE 3000 (p. 23), there is already an excellent standard (ISA 500) for when there is evidence that can be replicated directly to provide CSR report data. ISA 500 dictates that there must be adequate, suitable, and reliable evidence for the auditor to draw conclusions. As mentioned, the core concept of adequacy is related to the amount of evidence, suitability refers to the quality of the evidence, and reliability is affected by the source and nature of the evidence. The evidence should preferably be:

- from external sources
- controlled effectively
- direct and not inferences drawn from other material
- written
- original or in a form in which the audit trail will show any changes.

As already mentioned, if there are signs of weakness in the evidence, the auditor must increase the amount of evidence to increase the strength of the report's content, preferably using different methods and/or different sources, so that a statement with the desired degree of assurance can be established.

Data types

Just as there are degrees of verifiability in financial reporting, correspondingly, there are also degrees of verifiability in CSR reporting. This book makes the case that in the context of CSR reporting, companies work with two data types, which allow for different types of evidence. These data types are termed "documentable" and "probable".

Documentable data

The vast majority of CSR data can be proved very strongly: these are called "documentable data". The evidence can comprise documentation from a third party (invoices, delivery notes, pay slips, etc.) from, for example, the purchase of diesel or electricity, or timesheets. The company should ensure that these data are properly accrued just as the company does in the case of costs for financial reporting. Thus, the company ensures that CSR data are both valid and complete and that it maintains a link between financial reporting and CSR; in this way, the data have context and meaning.

Some verifiable data are measured locally using automatic or manual measurement equipment, which is a good start, but not in itself quite enough to ensure validity as the data do not come from an external source. The company will usually be able to take steps to improve the quality of these types of data and these can be used in combination:

- The company may have two independent persons perform the same measurements over the reporting period. These measurements can be checked against each other for verification. In the case of divergent measurements, the company should define in writing which of the measurements is most appropriate for use.

- The auditor can check and verify that automatic measurements are working.
- The company can employ one set of measurements, but this requires a subsequent analysis of the probability of error (divergence) relative to production or consumption norms. In the case of any deviations from the expected measurements, the company must document why it is retaining a measurement, or whether it has had to correct any measurements.

Data for CO_2 equivalents, energy, number of staff by gender and management, accidents, exposure hours of own employees, fatalities, external training hours, donations, and all governance data are documentable. These data can all be proved strongly and would therefore provide a basis for an ISAE 3000 reasonable (high) level statement.

Probable data

There are some data for which the company has no third party documentation and which the company might not even be able to measure. For example, such data may relate to water in countries where the company does not pay for the water and has no measuring equipment, or waste in the case in which the company does not pay for its disposal. Here, the company will have to use probability to ensure that the data are valid and complete. To the extent that the company has verifiable data, these data must be used as they are of the best quality: an example might be if the company has activities in northern Europe, where there is third party evidence for most of these matters, or the company itself may have installed measuring equipment of which the quality has been tested.

It is important that probable data can always be defended. The assumptions made to make such data plausible need to be recorded in writing in a memorandum and it must be possible for the auditor to make a presumption that the assumptions are valid. It may be that the company undertakes activities in Uganda, for example, where obtaining water is simply a matter of turning on a tap, but the company is not paying for it. Thus, if the company has no documentation such as invoices, or measuring equipment to establish the level of water consumption, then it makes sense for the company to obtain plausible data using the standard consumption of water for the given activity in this geographical location. Therefore, the company must identify the drivers of water use – for example, production volumes – whereby it is possible to show the probable level of water consumption. This is deduced evidence and is therefore weak, but it is evidence nonetheless. Due to their weaker probative value, these data will be able to carry an ISAE 3000 statement with limited assurance at best.

Typical probable data are water, waste, internal training hours, voluntary working hours, and exposure hours for contract staff.

In cases in which there are data of different evidentiary natures, one can see that the auditor/reviewer will need to choose to split the statement's assurance level between the documentable and probable data. This will assure all companies have comparable review of the minimum data, as the review level is given via the data types and is not down to the choice of an individual company.

Note

1   Engagement letters are sent by the auditor to the company's bank(s) to ensure all engagements the company may have with the bank(s) are revealed to the auditor; by this process the auditor tries to assure completeness about the bank information for the company, instead of solely relying on the statements presented by the company.

7

HOW TO CREATE A GOOD CONTROL ENVIRONMENT

After identifying the standard of evidence, we can now turn to devising ways in which the company can ensure that the control environment for CSR reporting is equal to that for financial reporting and will thus provide the evidence required for the data reported. Here, the focus is on how the company can ensure the control environment both locally and at the group level, as both elements must be in place to ensure the control environment is effective.

In the last 10 to 15 years, various solutions ensuring a good control environment have been developed throughout most of the world; some are relatively rigid (e.g. US Sarbanes Oxley (SOX) Act[1]) and some are more flexible (e.g. EuroSOX[2]). Most SOX compliance solutions require that publicly traded companies must disclose risk management activities in their annual reports. These include: procedures or systems the company has established in the context of risk management; how management regularly identifies and manages the risks of material misstatement in financial reporting and internal control systems; and what measures the company has put in place to ensure that significant errors in financial reporting can be detected, addressed, and corrected.

SOX legislation has meant that many large listed companies have established functions dedicated solely to addressing how to ensure an overview and strengthening of their control environments worldwide. This practice of ensuring the control environment surrounding the financial reporting process can usefully be replicated directly in CSR reporting so that the quality of data in the report can be guaranteed to be rooted locally. When the control environment for the CSR report is documented, a group's management can also confer a quality value on the CSR data, which is the basis for including the data in tactical and operational decision making. Finally, all things being equal, such a setup makes the role of the group's CSR data controller easier as the data providers disclose that all material controls, provision of evidence, and the monitoring of the controls have been carried out satisfactorily; this can result in a faster review progress and possibly lead to a smaller reviewer bill for the company.

Since the EU directives behind the so-called EuroSOX were passed in 2008, at least two generic methods have evolved in relation to compliance, i.e. the centralized and decentralized methods. The centralized method is characterized as particularly suitable for mono companies, which produce the same goods or services worldwide and have a shared Enterprise Resource Planning (ERP) system. Corporate enterprises of this sort can establish one set of controls that all companies in the group must implement and comply with. This very effective model also makes it possible for the group to follow up on any issues given the common set of controls.

The alternative is the decentralized method, which is characterized as suitable for groups that are conglomerates with very different business units and/or that have many different ERP systems around the globe. Companies of this type often need to establish a more decentralized approach in which the group defines a set of control objectives, and all the companies/business units in the group must at least establish controls to achieve these objectives and potentially also specific control objectives only related to their specific risks. The controls that the individual companies/business units establish for achieving these objectives are determined locally. Follow-up on the controls carried out is correspondingly more locally oriented. For the group to have an overview of all key controls there must also be some reporting to the group and follow-up of the fulfilment of the control objectives by the group, even when using the decentralized method.

Although these sound like two completely different methods, they are based on the same logic. This logic and the corresponding working methods and tools are presented in the following sections; it will become apparent that these can be deftly transferred to the CSR-reporting control environment, which will be in the interests of both company and its investors. This does not mean that the statement, which most SOX regulations require in the annual report, needs to be changed in any way as it is simply an extension of the control objectives to be achieved; of course, it must be reported to the audit committee and that is all it takes. This will provide valuable leverage to boards in CSR-reporting companies, if they are to sign the non-financial report. Hence, what the SOX legislation has done for the comfort of boards and to reassure the readers of financial reports could also easily be done for non-financial reports.

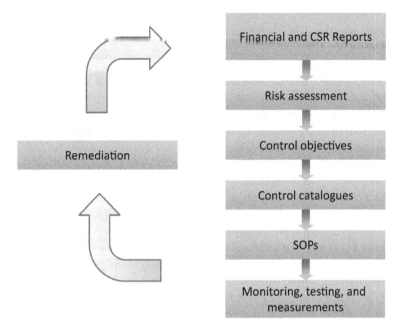

FIGURE 7.1 Annual process to ensure the control environment

Local work organization within a control environment

To ensure that SOX regulations are met, most listed companies have established a process such as that shown in Figure 7.1.

Regardless of the aforementioned methods, the process starts and ends at the headquarters and is performed at least annually. The model is to some extent inspired by the Committee of Sponsoring Organizations (COSO). However, companies often do not use the COSO model to the letter as it is a very comprehensive set of concepts. Even if a company simply follows the COSO conceptual framework in general terms, it must initiate the process by identifying risks, and based on this risk assessment, identify control objectives and activities; information and communication must then be disseminated concerning the controls. Finally, there must be monitoring to ensure that the controls are carried out as required. This sounds fairly logical and simple, and in fact it is relatively straightforward. In the following section, the individual sub-elements are described and practical examples of the tools are provided.

Risk assessment and control objectives

The process of risk assessment begins with a gross assessment of the underlying probability that elements in the report will be flawed and to what extent, if controls are not carried out. The risk assessment has two sets of inputs: first, a quantitative input from the reports of the impact from each reporting element, and second, a qualitative input concerning the probability of incorrect reporting for each reporting element.

In order to evaluate the quantitative input from each reporting element in relation to the report as a whole, the reporting element is put in context to assign relative values to the individual elements, i.e. how major/important is the element compared to the total reporting? When doing this financially, one often uses revenue figures, total assets, or cash flow from investing activities, for example, to assess whether the inventory is an essential item, and then make a comparison with total assets. One can undertake a similar process for CSR records, and in this context the company can again benefit greatly from the financial scoped data because these CSR elements can immediately be placed in the same financial context as the financial elements.

The qualitative input stems from several sources, for instance from external and internal auditors, from controllers, and/or from an overall assessment of the nature of the reporting element (e.g. are many or only a few estimates incorporated as an inherent part of this element?). Thus, financial provisions always have a high element of risk as they are based on estimates, whereas cash at bank typically represents a low qualitative risk as it is based on objective bank reconciliations. However, if auditors find that a specific company, for one reason or another, has difficulty performing sound bank reconciliations, the qualitative risk of cash at bank should be higher for that company. Similarly, it is possible to assess the CSR data qualitatively.

Typically, documentable data represent a lower qualitative risk than probable data. Of course, the company may have a history of being poor at assuring data that it should usually be possible to document fairly strongly (e.g. electricity consumption), and thus the qualitative risk will be higher for electricity reporting in this company. The qualitative assessment of each element is the basis for the control objectives, which are allocated to each reporting element. Therefore, it is important that the qualitative assessment is supported by a description of any possible problems that are known for the given element in this activity, which will enable the item being identified to be gauged. This will also make it easier to identify valid evidence of control.

Once the quantitative and qualitative risks have been identified individually, they should be paired so that the total risk per reported line item can be evaluated. This is typically undertaken using a table such as that shown in Table 7.1.

TABLE 7.1 Risk assessment of wrong reporting[a]

	% of revenue, staff cost or CO_2	*Quantitative impact on CSR report*	*Qualitative impact on CSR report*	*Total risk evaluation*
		H, M, L	H, M, L	1–5
CO_2-sources				
Oil	73%	High	Moderate	4
Gas	5%	Moderate	Moderate	3
Diesel	2%	Low	Moderate	2
Gasoline	7%	Moderate	Moderate	3
Kerosene	3%	Low	Moderate	2
Coal	0%	Low	Moderate	2
Biomass	1%	Low	Moderate	2
Electricity	5%	Moderate	Low	2
District heating	4%	Low	Low	1
CO_2-total	100%			
Other documentable data				
Energy from renewable energy source	1%	Low	Moderate	2
Number of employees (FTEs)	26%	High	Moderate	4
LTIs	3%	Low	Moderate	2
Exposure hours – own employees	n/a	High	Moderate	4
Fatalities	1%	Low	Moderate	2
External training hours	7%	Moderate	Low	2
Donations	1%	Low	Low	1
Governance data	n/a	High	Moderate	4
Probable data				
Water consumption	55%	High	High	5
Waste	12%	Moderate	High	4
Exposure hours – contract workers	3%	Low	High	3
Internal training hours	10%	Moderate	High	4
Voluntary work for community	2%	Low	High	3

a From this risk assessment, it is clear that in this incident there must be formalized controls for at least oil consumption, numbers of employees, exposure hours (own employees), governance data, water consumption, waste, and internal training hours

It can be seen from the table that in this company CO_2e is always in scope: the question is simply which CO_2e source(s) has(have) the greatest impact, calculated according to the different sources of impact on the overall CO_2e emissions. It is up to the company to determine whether specific controls concerning CO_2e should also apply to its business, but this is typically the case as almost all CSR-reporting companies include CO_2e as one of their most important indicators.

Next, it is noted that the quantitative impact of, for example, exposure hours for the company's own employees can be assessed via the number of FTEs, which again is given via the staff cost in relation to revenue.[3] This tends to make sense because these two elements are often closely related quantitatively: the greater the turnover, the longer employees are exposed to injuries and the more staff cost. However, this also depends on the kind of business in which the risk assessment is applied.

Finally, it is noted that governance data are not objectively assessed quantitatively but are judged to be of great importance to the content of the CSR report overall. Thus, the management description is assumed to be important in relation to how the company is considered to perform CSR.

The critical reader will object that this quantitative "measurement" is not based solely on the direct quantitative impact of various elements; rather, the situation is the same as for financial reporting, in which the company evaluates the quantitative risk using, for example, exchange rates, data transfer conditions, or contingent liabilities. These items are included without difficulty in the financial risk assessment, simply by assessing their impact in the financial statements "as such". This approach can also be adopted in the CSR context.

Risk assessment then takes place using simple arithmetic rules: 1 = low, 2 = moderate, 3 = high. The two scores for the quantitative and qualitative inputs are summed and one subtracted, so that the overall result of the assessment is as follows: 1 = low risk, 2–3 = moderate risk and 4–5 = high risk. The scores may be displayed in a more visual manner using a risk diagram (see Figure 7.2). High-risk elements should always be included in ongoing work to ensure the control environment as they are considered to be essential.

In a centralized model, only one group-based risk assessment is undertaken and this then applies to all reporting units in the group. In a decentralized model, the risk assessment from the group only provides a set of minimum control objectives and it is then up to the different reporting business units to carry out their own risk assessment, drawing on their own input. The local risk assessments can lead to additional control objectives; however, reporting units cannot disregard the group's minimum requirements, unless a reporting element does not apply to them at all (because the reporting unit does not have any of the reporting element, e.g. FTEs in a holding company with no staff).

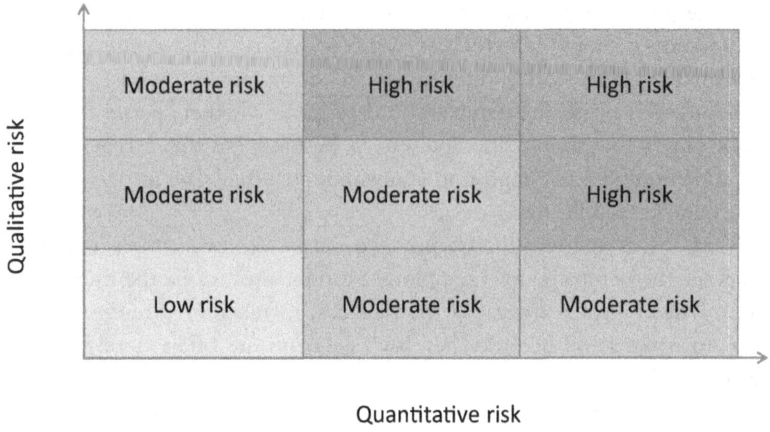

FIGURE 7.2 Risk diagram

Control catalogues

Having undertaken the risk assessment and identified the reporting elements to be included in the monitored control environment, it is then time for the company to identify which controls should be put in place to mitigate the risks and achieve the identified control objectives. As there are typically several controls, it is helpful to gain an overview of the controls per reporting element. This is usually undertaken using a "control catalogue" containing the following information per control:

- the risk identified to be mitigated
- the control objectives identified
- an indication of whether the control objectives are relevant to the reporting entity (e.g. if the company does not use heating at all, it should not implement controls for heating measurements)
- a brief description of control activity
- an identification of the evidence that the controls are carried out with satisfactory outcomes
- a reference to a more detailed description of the controls, i.e. Standard Operating Procedures (SOPs)
- a reference to where evidence of the control activities is stored (which also provides very useful information for the auditor/reviewer)
- identification of the type of controls (detective or preventive; manual or automatic)
- control frequency – how often controls are performed
- control owner (whoever has defined the controls and related evidence)

- control performer (often someone other than the control owner)
- control maturity, i.e. how well the control is implemented, typically on a scale (e.g. 0–5; see the maturity decision tree in Figure 7.3)
- a remediation plan with deadlines and the identification of responsible person(s), if control maturity is not sufficiently high compared to the group's requirements.

As mentioned, one of the key elements of a control catalogue is that the maturity of the individual control is assessed. This could be done using a "maturity decision tree" (see Figure 7.3).

When using the decision tree to assess the maturity of a control, one should start at the top of the decision tree and work downwards through the questions. For example, a company may well have an automated control which will remain only at maturity level 2 if there is no description of the control in a SOP. It should be stressed that it is not necessarily a goal that all controls be automated. In fact, it is often the controls that involve manual estimates that are more difficult; hence the qualitative risks of such controls are higher than the relatively easier controls such as metering, which can more easily be automated.

The self-assessed control maturity of a local reporting entity must be monitored to ensure that control descriptions, evidence, and the frequency

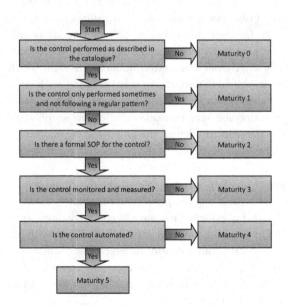

FIGURE 7.3 Maturity decision tree for controls

of entries in the control catalogue provide a true picture of what is happening. Often companies use internal audit functions or controller functions for this kind of review. However, a group can also reuse external auditors/ reviewers' management letters, internal audits, and/or group controllers' reports of errors found, to indicate or evaluate whether the reporting entity may have been a little too generous in relation to self-assessed maturities. This means that the group can, to some extent, reuse auditing actions that have already been performed to validate and substantiate descriptions of the control environment. Thus, establishing a good control environment is not just extra work, as the company can reuse monitoring already carried out in a new context – though it will often need a specific internal supplement. After the "pressure test" of the self-assessed maturity assessments, the company can show how large a gap there is between the qualified and the self-assessed maturity of the reporting entity, a gap that can be termed the "uprightness gap". This gap must obviously be reported to the group's audit committee so that it knows what value it can attach to other information from the reporting entity.

Another element that may be evaluated is the quality of the controls. If you use the centralized method, it means that the group determines which controls are to be implemented throughout the entire group. It also means that the group has already taken a position in terms of which controls it is appropriate to use from a quality perspective. For a group that works with the centralized principles, it is only the local maturity of these controls that can be the basis for discussion between the reporting entity and the group, not the quality. However, if the organization uses the decentralized method, the group only determines minimum control objectives for which local controls must be established to mitigate the risks identified. Each reporting entity must then decide which control(s) will be implemented to meet the control objectives. This decision may be made more or less soundly and therefore, in addition to the maturity debate, the group and the reporting entity may also have a debate on the quality of the control that the reporting entity has taken on.

A frequent error when it comes to ensuring the completeness of an item is the test direction as it requires proof from outside the "book" to meet the control objective, i.e. evidence not already recorded, often stemming from third parties. The intuitive approach, especially for those without a financial background, is to carry out a control in which the company reviews what is already registered, which does not ensure completeness; at best it confers only validity, but the control does not actually meet the objective and thus the quality of the control is very low.

In cases in which the quality of the local controls must be evaluated, it would be appropriate for all parties to the communication to evaluate the control catalogue for each and every reporting entity, if the group uses a known indisputable quality scale, not least when reporting to the audit committee. This ensures a consistent method that can be consolidated across the reporting units. The scale could be as follows:

0 = nothing submitted
1 = the submission does not cover the control objective (this often happens when control is turned upside down and does not test completeness, which is the most difficult situation)
2 = control activity and the evidence are not specified
3 = control activity or the evidence is not specified
4 = a little fine tuning/specification is necessary, but the substance is satisfactory
5 = OK.

Quality must be assessed both in the control catalogue and in the SOP (see the next section). This can help to establish an overall quality score for all controls. By combining quality control with the maturity of controls and setting this total score against the initially assessed risk of misstatement, the group has a good picture of the net risk of error. Of course, the net risk per control objective must also be reported to the audit committee and could be as represented in Figure 7.4, for example.

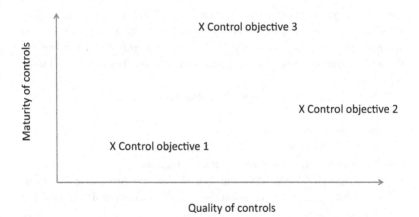

FIGURE 7.4 Overview of the control environment per control objective

The chart provided in Figure 7.4 shows that control objective 1 has both quality problems and issues with the implementation of controls, whereby the identified control objectives are most probably not being achieved. Control objective 2 is of excellent quality but low maturity, i.e. the ideas for the controls are sufficient, but the reporting unit now needs to implement them completely. Finally, control objective 3 shows good implementation, but the quality of the controls leaves something to be desired. These three different outcomes will call on three very different activities to be undertaken to improve the control environment to meet the control objectives. This list is also useful for showing progress as it is possible to include directional arrows, whereby the audit committee may be able to see developments in the control environment.

Standard Operating Procedures (SOPs)

When the control catalogue (which only serves as an overview of the controls) has been established, it is time to develop more specific SOPs. These are important, not only because they often act as a kind of workflow description, but also because they ensure that the selected control is performed in the same way across the organization. A typical error in SOPs occurs if the reporting entity only uses existing process descriptions as these too often do not contain control activity descriptions and even more rarely do they identify the evidence for that the control was executed and provided a valid outcome. Existing SOPs are rarely created with the purpose of describing the control workflow, but that is the most important aspect in this context. The company can easily reuse existing process descriptions if the control activity/description and the specification and evidence are given at least in an appendix. Thus, the company does not need to start from scratch, but can use what is already there (assuming all is otherwise well) and then add what is missing.

A SOP should contain at least the following elements:

- the SOP's name
- the SOP's reference in the control catalogue
- the version number and date of the last revision
- the purpose of the SOP, i.e. the control objective (by asking "what can go wrong?" one can understand the control objective and often also the requisite evidence)
- who or what job function performs the control
- the frequency of the control

- the process description (possibly also with a process flowchart)
- a description of control activity
- identification of evidence that the control is performed with a satisfactory outcome, potentially exemplified so that the SOP can rigorously show what valid evidence should look like.

If the centralized method is followed, it is only necessary to produce one set of SOPs that everyone in the whole group has to follow worldwide. Conversely, if the decentralized method is employed, each reporting entity has to produce a set of SOPs equivalent to the controls each has identified and established in its control catalogue. Thus, the considerable freedom a reporting entity has in the decentralized model to decide for itself in terms of how it wants to operate, is associated with an equally important responsibility to describe its specific processes and controls so that the group can obtain the required overview of all key controls throughout the group globally, both financially and non-financially.

Monitoring

Having identified and described the significant risks and consequent controls in both summary form and in detail, it is time to monitor the controls: are they actually performed as intended? Only when this is verified will the group audit committee honestly be able to declare that it has a real overview of the company's control environment, and not before.

This is often the part of the control environment that is problematic in terms of providing an explanation, because is this monitoring not a little like heaping sugar on sugar? Is it really necessary to verify that the control has been exercised? Control frameworks such as US-SOX 404 are often blamed for testing for testing's sake, as well as being the most expensive and perhaps the least efficient part of the assurance of the control environment. However, monitoring is important in order to guarantee the significance of the reported control environment; the group can then be confident not only in claims by local units that everything is in perfect order, but also that there is substance behind their claims, and not least that instances in which processes might lag slightly are identified. It is necessary to ensure that processes are effective, but monitoring can be made more or less efficient. As has been pointed out a few times previously, the company can choose to reuse monitoring controls already conducted as part of the monitoring process, saving both time and money. Thus, the internal and external auditors' reports can be used as important indicators, and it is also important to collect information concerning mistakes reported by group controllers. Together, these reports provide a clear indication of which controls do not work, are not performed, or are performed incorrectly.

In addition, the company can also choose to undertake a process in which reporting entities perform parts of the monitoring themselves. The cheapest method is to send questionnaires to the local units. The second cheapest is "desktop solutions", in which the group/reporting entity asks the local unit to submit evidence of a given control. Finally, there is the expensive version, in which designated personnel visit the local units; this is a solution which often cannot stand alone, as it is rare that all local units in large corporations can be visited in a year. The optimal option is a combination of at least two of the aforementioned methods, thus ensuring that monitoring not only consists of self-assessment, but also is an appropriate measure of the procedures undertaken by the entire company. Such monitoring should be the basis for establishing the level of maturity that is reported in the control catalogue.

For the sometimes extensive work of monitoring, many software systems have been developed that can provide excellent results, but these can also be large scale and expensive, not to mention cumbersome to work with. Such systems are often onerous because they are usually designed as central databases to keep track of, for example, which specific employees of company X in Uganda and company Y in Japan are performing each control activity, so that these employees (or their bosses) are reminded to perform certain controls. As the astute reader will observe, for a large multinational corporation with many companies in the group, it will be a full-time job just keeping track of whether personnel in Uganda, Japan, and the rest of the world remain in their respective jobs and that they are not suddenly assigned to new tasks, or are no longer employed by the company. In the latter cases, there is the issue of who has then taken over the tasks of measuring electricity and water consumption. The entire process is expensive and time consuming. However, the excellent aspect of the software systems developed is that they can often provide evidence in a central location so that SOPs and other information are updated. On the other hand, a major drawback of such systems is that they are often employed as "box-ticking" exercises, in which the employees, who must report to the system more or less aimlessly every month, simply respond "yes" to everything, rather than providing genuine updates, because it is faster and generates fewer questions from headquarters. It is therefore very important that the company decides whether it is willing to place such a relatively large administrative burden on local units and the group per se, or whether it should seek a somewhat simpler solution, for example, employing Microsoft's SharePoint libraries/lists or an equivalent, which may only need to be completed occasionally, thus avoiding the "box-ticking" circus.

Headquarter tasks to ensure the control environment

Just as there are controls to be carried out locally, so of course there are also a number of controls that should be carried out by the headquarters, so that the control environment and thus the data can be guaranteed to be of a certain quality. Furthermore, it is also the task of the headquarters to make reporting tools available so that audit trails can be maintained for group reporting.

Software selection

The headquarters must ensure that the company is using a proper consolidation tool that can be IT-reviewed/audited: Microsoft's Excel is not an option for this purpose. For various reasons, many companies have decided to use Excel for their CSR consolidation. Although Excel is a favourite financial tool that has many benefits, it is not a consolidation tool. In particular it has the following disadvantages:

- Excel cannot assure the audit trail, as all cells can of course be changed continuously. This means that you cannot track what the data were yesterday compared to what they are now, or how and why the data were changed, not least by whom.
- Excel is a tool for individual use. The company quickly becomes dependent on the individual who has developed the spreadsheet, which is an unnecessary risk for the company. We have all tried to take over someone else's spreadsheet and it can be extremely difficult to be sure that you have understood all the formulas and any macros in the spreadsheet. It is more useful to work with a tool that is better known and documented both internally and externally, and for which there is also an externally validated manual and training, as there is with an actual consolidation tool.
- It is difficult to work with cross-ownership and ownership-by-period in Excel, which is important when the group buys and sells all or parts of legal entities. Consolidation tools are designed for just such circumstances.

However, in addition to addressing the already mentioned disadvantages of Excel, if non-financial and financial colleagues can agree to work in tandem with the financial data so that CSR data are also collected using whatever software is employed as the regular financial consolidation tool, the company can achieve the following benefits:

- The solution is virtually free: the system is already available, it is already being taught in use, there are user manuals, and an IT audit has already been made. It only requires that metadata are expanded with a CSR nomenclature. This is a manageable task, and takes a very short amount of time.
- There is a well-established user access control and the system is already available to all companies in the group. The local financial staff will be familiar with the system in advance, so – if nothing else – they can help local CSR employees report the data. This creates a good new dynamic between the two groups of staff, who should know each other's worlds due to the likely future demand for integrated reporting.
- It is possible to reuse ownership and segment structure automatically. Thus, it is already assured that with this tool all companies and each activity in the group are covered, just as is the case financially. This assures financial boundaries.
- There is full visibility between the individual company financial data and CSR data, which can help assure the control framework for CSR data completeness.
- Typically, such systems also bring opportunities in terms of ensuring, for example, a consistent calculation of the CO_2 equivalents at all levels of the company.

In addition to the above, there is a plethora of customized CSR-reporting systems. These are often hugely expensive and can take a very long time to implement. Generally, it is also the case that these solutions do not confer some of the benefits that the use of the existing consolidation tool provides. In particular, it is very difficult to undertake consolidation correctly using such systems if the company has many cross-ownerships and/or joint operations that are to be consolidated pro rata; this is because these systems are typically designed to work within operational boundaries and consolidation since everything is consolidated 100 percent. The only thing these systems are really good at is converting from one unit to the common unit of measurement (e.g. from kWh to GJ)[4] and this is quite unique compared to the classic consolidation tools. Given that the group can simply set conversion standards as given in Appendix E, and share these with all its legal entities, the question then is whether the facility for unit conversion is argument enough for not deploying the other benefits of the existing consolidation tool, which are essentially free of charge.

Logical group controls

It is clear that there must be local reviews to ensure that the data reported are underpinned by evidence, as indicated earlier. However, just as with financial reporting, the control team at headquarters should also ensure that the data contained in the reports make sense per reporting unit and that they can be explained at group level. Thus, when data are collected per legal entity per activity and signed off by business unit managers, it is time for the group to verify that the data are valid and complete so that it is possible to conclude the group review. For this, common sense and logic are needed, not to mention a considerable amount of common controlling work at headquarters. The following controls all have in common the fact that they can only be performed if it has been ensured that the CSR data are collated in accordance with financial boundaries and financial consolidation.

In this process, one starts by ensuring that all legal entities have delivered. Even the smallest of offices have to contribute to the CSR report, just as they do financially. It creates good morale within the organization if the CSR report is treated with the same respect as the financial report. It also means that all the financial rules on signatures, deviation reports, etc., must also apply to CSR reporting. Thus, there should be an explanation sheet for each reporting unit covering the developments in all CSR indicators. This makes it much simpler to prepare group explanations for the development of the data and confers greater transparency.

For each legal entity the following aspects should be considered for each activity:

- Are there staff costs? If so, there should also be FTEs.[5] If there are FTEs, there should be data on at least electricity, water, and waste. There should also be exposure hours and LTIs, but only to the extent that employees are working on or by the company's assets according to financial boundaries. There may also be heating consumption of one sort or another, but this depends on geography.
- Typically, there should be some logic in terms of minimum consumption and exposure hours per FTE or output – sometimes afforded by geography (e.g. the use of electricity per FTE in North America is significantly higher than anywhere else in the world, and exposure hours differ depending on the standard times for work locally). As mentioned earlier,

the company can benefit from establishing geographical office standards which can indicate logical minimum consumption. In this way it is possible to control for any reporting that appears skewed, which could be the result of improper use of units and/or incomplete/invalid boundaries.

- If the company obtains financial information on the costs of fuel, electricity, or district heating, then there should also be corresponding consumption volumes. Hence, there should also be a test to ensure that the relationship between cost and volume makes sense; this can detect skewed units.

- The company should test whether the electricity and district heating provisions make sense for the given country. If the legal entity is resident in Sweden, it is not likely that the entity will purchase electricity from South Africa. However, it can happen. One cannot assume that the home country is always the source of electricity or district heating. The reporting of the country of purchase has an impact on which consumption converters should be used to recalculate to CO_2 equivalents, as different countries use different fuels to produce electricity and district heating. For example, emissions in Iceland are zero due to its geothermal sources of energy.

- If the company owns or has leased machinery or vehicles there should also be an equivalent use of fuels or electricity. One should of course deduct the assets leased out in this logical analysis. The connection can be tested by pulling non-current tangible assets from the financial data and adding net operating leases (operating leases in minus leases out – all of which can be found in the Profit & Loss (P&L)); this exercise gives an overview of the machinery and transport equipment which are available for the company's production and sales, and which should be read in conjunction with CSR data for fuels and electricity. In any case, an explanation should be required if there is machinery/transport equipment with a book value which is not leased out and apparently not used (deduced because there is no consumption of fuels and/or electricity), and therefore of no value to the company's production. Perhaps the CSR report and/or the financial report are not quite right.

- Some activities will almost always generate hazardous waste. If the group engages in this kind of activity, it should ensure that the quantities of hazardous waste are logical in relation to the production quantities.

Thus, one can go a fair way in group control by means of simple logic. When the group deviation report is complete, it is time to calculate and/or recalculate CO_2 equivalents, both for the group and business units. As mentioned, this process can be undertaken through the consolidation system, but it can also be done after the data are consolidated and extracted in relation to trial balances in the report. If the calculations are done outside the consolidation system it is important that all fuel inventories are reconciled beforehand. After executing this set of controls, the auditor may perform the final review of the data, calculations, and explanations of development.

Notes

1   The Sarbanes Oxley (SOX) Act is US legislation aimed at securing processes in accounting and financial reporting. The 404 designation refers to a specific section of the SOX Act of 2002 which addresses the assessment of internal control. SOX was established based on the Enron scandal and is both highly criticised as being difficult, bureaucratic, and expensive, and praised for actually having reduced the amount of fraud.

2   Although the term "EuroSOX" is commonly used, it is perhaps not the best name for several reasons, not least because it has little to do with the US-SOX 404: the European law is simply far too vague for that. Furthermore, for some reason, certain Nordic countries have allowed private persons to patent the name; therefore, some companies have chosen to call it something quite different, for example, Internal Control and Risk Management (ICRM) or Risk & Control Compliance (RICC).

3   $x < 5$ percent = low, $5 < x < 20$ percent = moderate, $x > 20$ percent = high.

4   This can also be done using a consolidation tool, but it usually requires a little massaging of the system as it cannot be done as easily as with the currency conversion of an entire legal entity report, but must be made per account per legal entity.

5   FTEs clearly have to tally between the financial and the CSR reports. This is most easily done by collecting the data set only once and then sharing it between the two reports. Thus, it is necessary to ensure the FTE data collection includes a split between gender and management levels as indicated in the section on social data (p. 67) in Chapter 5 "Proposed minimum data". Then the data set also works for the staff-cost note in the financial report.

8
HOW CAN INVESTORS USE CSR IN THEIR ANALYSIS OF STOCKS?

A minimum set of CSR data has been defined and how these data should be validated and presented in uniform ESG notes has also been described. But how should investors use these data? Investors have the opportunity to put money into thousands of investment objects; thus, to be able to make sound, valid choices, they must be able to analyze the performance of several thousand companies in one go. It is therefore significantly more useful for investors if companies' CSR performance can be quantified and presented in uniform notes which investors know where to find, as well as what to look for. Some will probably oppose this claim, and will maintain that a qualitative report is just as effective as a quantitative one in order to detect a trend. The problem is, though, that such reports cannot be used by investors – no matter how fine and creative they are. They are simply not useful when the investor must make large comparative analyses for investment decisions. But what will it take for the investor to involve CSR in investment considerations? According to Birgitte Mogensen, former partner at PWC:

> Investors must with figures be able to tell the difference between the various entities' CSR work. That means that the reporting on CSR performance must be with specific non-financial key ratios… Only when investors and their financial analysts can recognize CSR performance in their stock assessment models will CSR…play a role in the share trade.[1]

Why should companies measure their CSR? We know, as mentioned earlier in the book, that the investor can benefit from better understanding the risk profile of the business, and that this insight can be ensured through CSR reporting on environmental, social, and governance conditions. If these data can be made even more useful for both investors and companies, then one can imagine that different ratios will be developed – especially the kind of ratios that combine CSR and financial data, which will be immediately useful. These figures may well give the investor a better understanding of the links between production, environmental and social conditions, and thus the company's risk profile.

Triple Bottom Line

As early as the mid-1990s, John Elkington led a discussion on combining these data sets in what was called the Triple Bottom Line (TBL),[2] which sought to combine the economic, social, and environmental bottom lines – called the 3 Ps: People, Planet and Profit. It is not clear from Elkington's ideas which economic bottom line he was referring to, something which has been, and continues to be, the subject of much debate among economists. Similarly, the environmental and social bottom lines are also very loosely defined. The big problem for TBL is, of course, in addition to its loose definitions, the resolution of the question of how to get to a common unit, whereby the three bottom lines can be summed up – e.g. the US dollar.

Many attempts have since been made to calculate an actual TBL and, for example, SABMiller and Novo Nordisk have for many years been front-runners in this exercise. If one looks at a SABMiller's statement of TBL, it looks like it is just a reorganization of the regular cash-flow[3] note from the financial annual report, of which many companies have actually made similar versions (Figure 8.1).

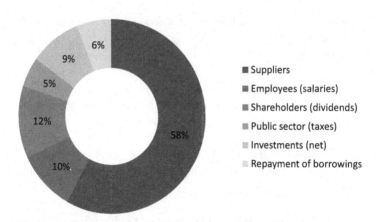

FIGURE 8.1   Cash outflow distribution

Thus, with this reorganized cash-flow note one can see how the cash out-flow from the company goes variously to employees, public sector, suppliers, investors, investments, loans, etc. Most qualified analysts, if they want to, should be able to prepare a similar note using the regular annual reports, including for those companies that do not yet reorganize their cash-flow notes. However, it is not clear how this should provide better insight into the company, its contribution to society, or its risk profile. Is the company good at distributing money out of the company, and is that important? How well do the competitors do this – are they better at distributing cash outflow than their competitors – and what is good? Is equitable distribution a valid goal? Or maybe a better focus would be on employees or investors always having a certain proportion of the outflow? We do not know what good this reorgan-ized cash-flow model does, since discussion of the meaning and evaluation of such a reorganized cash-flow note is missing.

But maybe this reorganized cash-flow note could be the first step in cre-ating elements of an alternative integrated note that could be based on the IIRC[4] principles with reference to the input-activities-output-outcome model and all the identified "capitals". Maybe the regular financial cash-flow model should, in this context, be reorganized from:[5]

> cash flow from operating activities + cash flow from investing activities + cash flow from financing activities = net increase/decrease in cash and cash equivalents

to:

> cash inflow + cash outflow = net increase/decrease in cash and cash equivalents

where:

> cash inflow = capital injections + loans from externals + customer payments + divestitures + net financial income received

> cash outflow = staff cost paid + suppliers paid + dividends paid + invest-ments paid + loans to externals or repaid loans + paid taxes + donations paid.

Cash inflow could then be assigned to Input and cash outflow to Outcome.[6] It could also be argued that the regular financial cash flow, as defined by

IASB, could be used as it is and no reorganization is needed, and all should be included in the Outcome, as all the cash flows are the results of the activities going on in the company. That debate is necessary. But see Appendix G to see a suggestion for a new integrated note using this logic.

Some would in fact argue that the current CSR reporting in all CSR reporting companies, regardless of integration, is exactly TBL, even if there is no composite bottom line. Others[7] believe that TBL is merely part, or an extension, of the concepts of the Balanced Scorecard[8] (BSC) to something called the Sustainable Balanced Scorecard (SBSC). BSC is a performance-measurement method that some companies use as a tool to distribute bonus rewards for their employees and/or managers. BSC consists typically of key figures in finance, internal processes, customer/market and learning/development: examples are productivity, market share, new markets, research and development/sales. With SBSC the idea is to extend the calculation using social and environmental indicators, such as employee satisfaction and water consumption/production unit. The idea is that all the ratios that have been selected are measured and compared to last year, a budget, and/or competitors at scales ranging from 1 to 5. An average is calculated over each theme whereby measurement can be made of how the company and the individual manager/employee perform in the selected areas. The company can, on top of this, then decide what weighting the different themes must have for bonuses. Since all of this is calculated as part of internal reporting, it has little direct value for the investor; therefore this idea cannot be used in the context of investors. But it can probably be used internally.

In recent years there have been a few – very interesting – trials to convert some of the indicators, particularly those that are environmental, to a monetary unit through which, perhaps, Elkington's original idea on TBL is a bit closer to becoming a reality; companies might want to try such conversions for the following reasons:[9]

- in order to normalize the definition of the value
- to ensure that the evaluation of companies (including their environmental and social importance) can be compared
- to ensure that the significance of environmental and/or social problems can be evaluated.

In 2011, PUMA (which is part of the French luxury, clothes, and lifestyle company PPR Home) carried out an experiment based on their 2010 accounting and CSR reporting.[10] Here, they tried to establish what they called an E-P&L (Environmental Profit & Loss Account), using a conversion

of CO_2 emissions and water consumption to a euro-value via CO_2 allow-
ance prices and an average water price covering the whole world. In their
measurements, they not only included scope 1 and 2 emissions and con-
sumptions, but also input from those of their suppliers who had PUMA
as their main customer (meaning that at least 90 percent of the suppliers'
production was for PUMA), as well as their suppliers (subsuppliers) and subcontractors, and requested all these suppliers, subsuppliers and subcontractors
provide information about their fuel, electricity, and water consumption.[11]
Then PUMA converted the environmental impact of the PUMA production to a total amount of euros. Unfortunately, the calculation is not very
interesting, because PUMA did not relate the result to their own production or profits, but spent the rest of the report splitting the total amount of
euros geographically, which did not make much sense. But what makes the
calculation interesting per se is the fact that it is one of the first – if not the
first – in which a company has made progress in creating a common unit
that could have been used to gain an overview of the environmental impact
of producing its products. PUMA have since expanded the equation to also
include waste, air pollution, and the use of land[12] and have divided the environmental impact by product (i.e. footwear, apparel, and accessories). But no
relationship has yet been established between this information and PUMA's
financial results or production volumes. Table 8.1 shows the euro standards
that PUMA, along with TruCost and PWC, defined for the year 2010.

TABLE 8.1 PUMA's euro standards for environmental impact, 2010

Standards for environmental impact		Value in euros
Consumption of land	Per hectare	347
Air pollution	Particles (per metric tonne)	14,983
	Ammonia (per metric tonne)	1,673
	Sulphur dioxide (per metric tonne)	2,077
	Nitrogen oxides (per metric tonne)	1,186
	Various organic substances (per metric tonne)	836
Waste	Landfill (per metric tonne)	73
	Incineration (per metric tonne)	51
	Recycling (per metric tonne)	0
Water	Per m³	0.81
CO_2e	Per CO_2e tonnes	66

http://about.puma.com/puma-completes-first-environmental-profit-and-loss-account-which-
values-impacts-at-e-145-million/

The above is obviously a first step towards the possibility of measuring the environmental impact in a more homogeneous form, which is easier to communicate, and which an investor could effectively include in a relatively simple way in the calculations of whether a given stock is desirable or not. The model can be fairly easily expanded to include standards for the social area, such as the value of lack of safety (fatalities and injuries),[13] lack of diversity in the management layer (e.g. opportunity cost as a result of a lack of diversity), or the cost of having poor corporate governance (e.g. in terms of lack of audit committee, seniority of the board, and/or audit inequality in the board[14]). All three areas in the ESG – but especially the social area and governance – require that research becomes much more rigorous in terms of whether these issues are significant for company profitability; if they are indeed significant, their impact will then need to be identified in order to ensure development of generic economic standards for the meaning of these ESG parameters – preferably via use of meta-analyses, so validity is good. But most of this work can only be done when CSR reporting reaches a level of quality equal to that of the financial data.

Combined KPIs

The above indicated standards can be used to calculate a wide range of ratios, which could be used both for in-depth analysis of an individual company and, of course, for comparative analyses of many companies. Thus, for example, one could calculate something that might be called Return on Pollution (ROP) as a variant of Return on Invested Capital (ROIC). ROP is thus a measure of how much profit the company has made from polluting. It may sound a little backwards – most companies have no wish to pollute – so this ratio should be seen as an indicator of how to make the most profit by polluting as little as possible. This ratio is as industry-specific as ROIC, where investment demands are very different for an office that performs services, and a factory where the assets, and thus investment, are very heavy. Similarly, pollution is also very industry-specific.

ROP can be measured as follows:

(continuing operation profit after tax but before deduction of minority interests)/pollution.

Pollution must be measured in the currency that is also used to calculate the result (according to the method described by PUMA), and given the minimum data described in Chapter 5 "Proposed minimum data" and Appendix G, it can be calculated by using:

(CO_2e tonnes × CO_2 quotation price) + (water × generic water price) + (waste per year per destination type × generic waste rate per destination type).

It is noted that pollution data can only be scope 1 and 2 – i.e. the pollution directly attributable to the company's production. Scope 3 is simply too vague a concept and one that cannot be compared between companies; it therefore should not be included.

One can also imagine not using recalculation to a common unit as shown by the PUMA example. As previously indicated, it should be relatively easy to show, for example, CO_2 emissions or water consumption per produced unit. One can also imagine comparing EBIT or net profit with safety data, numbers of FTEs, or something else. In these cases the ratios are also very industry-specific.

Returning to the initial requirement in this book, namely that the investor can use CSR reporting as some kind of indicator of the risks of a company's operations, then one can imagine that the investor could combine this idea with classic specific investment ratios à la Price Earnings (P/E). CSR could be part of the forward-looking calculation/evaluation the investor must make in terms of a buy, sell, or hold disposition – CSR reporting can indicate whether, in addition to the financial return, there must also be an "insurance fee" for the investor, because the company pollutes too much and/or has social or governance challenges. We could add the values of all the suggested minimum data into a single unit, which we could call the CSR factor, and calculate this CSR factor per share. Next, place this CSR per share against the share price, and then you get P/CSR. P/CSR will be the opposite of the ordinary P/E value, since the CSR factor measures all the CSR-related discrepancies in the company – as opposed to E, which measures the earnings, which investors appreciate. This means that for a company to be attractive to investors, the size of the CSR factor should be reduced relative to the share price, but the P/CSR must still be compared with earnings relative to the share price: they must be seen together. So we cannot work with P/CSR without a P/E value – it is simply too naive to imagine that the economy does not mean anything to the investor. If we combine P/E with P/CSR, then the investors' assessment should follow the logic set out in Figure 8.2.

As can be seen, the P/CSR is of particular importance for the investor when assessing that part of investment opportunities that have moderate financial potential. One can rarely imagine that the evaluation of a financially really bad investment will be significantly differently assessed, regardless of how many CSR initiatives the company takes; in contrast, a company with high CSR risks could still be assessed to be at least moderately favourable

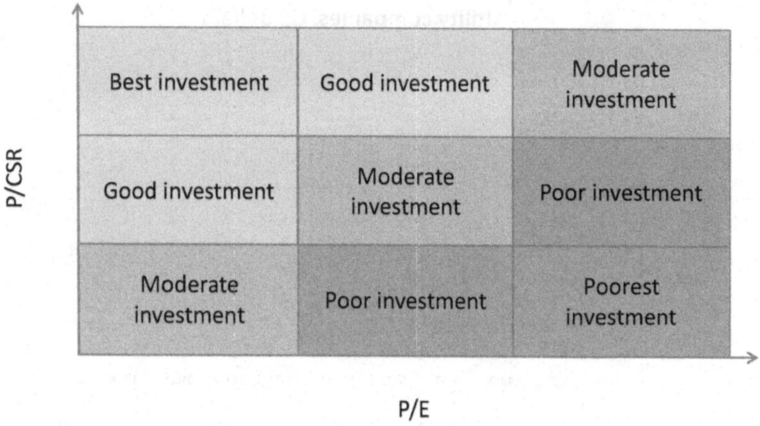

Best investment	Good investment	Moderate investment
Good investment	Moderate investment	Poor investment
Moderate investment	Poor investment	Poorest investment

P/E

FIGURE 8.2 P/E versus P/CSR – the investor logical tool

if it had good financial potential. Since the research has not yet reached the defined standards for elements of the social and governance areas, we cannot currently calculate P/CSR but must make do with calculating only Price Pollution (P/Pollution), where Pollution is measured in monetary units, which resembles the method described by PUMA. When there is more generic research based on valid and complete business data it will be possible to include these, so at some point it will be possible to measure the whole CSR factor.

With this model and a data set provided by CDP on the 2012 data[15] of the Global 500 companies (the 500 companies performing the best given CDP's measurements), it can be shown how this intertwining of classic investor KPIs with CSR data could be done and used. But first some data-cleaning is needed to secure data discipline: the Global 500 reports from CDP consist only of 83 reports done with financial boundaries; 11 of these have not been reviewed, and seven have not used the same period as that for their financial reporting. This leaves 65 reports that we can use for this analysis. The rest of the companies have, as argued earlier, provided data that cannot be compared with the financial data, and must therefore be ignored. Of these 65 reports, five have negative P/E values, and therefore they will be left out (not because of poor data quality, but due to negative financial performance). Of the remaining 60 valid reports, seven are from companies within the utility industry, and their P/E values from 2011 are quite similar. Therefore, is it interesting to assess the impact for the investor if something simple as

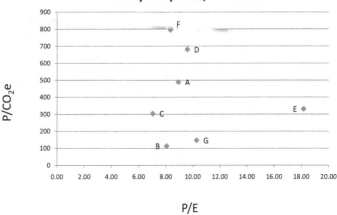

Utility companies, US dollars

FIGURE 8.3 P/E versus P/CO_2e for utility companies on CDP's Global 500 reports

share price/CO_2e per share (we can call that P/CO_2e) is included in the investment analysis (see Figure 8.3).[16]

If we only looked at this financially, we would probably suggest investing in C, since its P/E value is lowest[17] – that means the price per share compared to the earnings per share is the lowest. But when combined with P/CO_2e it becomes obvious that the risk of CO_2 pollution is far greater with this share compared with F, where the P/E is only slightly higher but the P/CO_2e is 200–300 percent higher. Given this combined analysis, the investor should potentially instead consider choosing to put their money in F, since the financial output is almost the same, but the CO_2 risks are significantly smaller.

Now, let us step closer to these two companies: F versus C. Both companies are relatively old and were originally 100 percent state-owned; however, over time, as the respective countries and the EU have liberalized the utility-providing industries, both have grown into international companies – though both are still controlled by their states, as well as being publicly traded companies. F primarily focuses on the northern countries, the Baltic states and Russia, while C is active in the central and southern parts of Europe and South America. C is approximately four times bigger than F production-wise, but seven to eight times bigger revenue-, cash-flow- and FTE-wise. Thus, on the one hand it can be concluded that C is getting a far better price per TWh, but on the other hand the TWh is twice as labour-intensive in C as in F.

But why is there such a big difference in their CO_2 risk profile, while their P/E values are somewhat alike? Looking at their production information, the first thing that becomes apparent is that in 2011 47 percent of F's production stemmed from nuclear power, which explains why its CO_2 emissions are significantly lower than those of C, who only had a share of 13 percent from its nuclear power plants. But using nuclear power will of course also produce other long-term waste issues and other kinds of pollution risks apart from the CO_2e emissions, just as the water consumption is higher than with regular power production. Finally, C has moved into the gas exploration industry to mitigate some of the risks of lack of gas delivery. All these elements should additionally be considered when evaluating the environmental risks of these shares.

Safety-wise we cannot compare the companies, as they report quite differently on this matter.

Looking at the two companies' governance, it is also obvious they are driven somewhat differently even though they have similarities (e.g. C does not have any women on the board of directors, while F has three women in a board of seven). But both companies have audit committees and make corporate governance statements, though they are quite different and not easily comparable. Both companies also produce CSR reports, which are reviewed by an auditor – both combining ISAE 3000 with limited assurance with AA1000 with reasonable assurance on AA1000APS – and, as mentioned, both are on CDP's Global 500, but only C is part of Forbes Fortune 500 and included in the Dow Jones Sustainability index.

Hence, the choice of where to invest may be a bit more complicated than just looking at financial aspects and potentially just looking at a ranking in an ESG index. This more integrated way of looking at the companies with more specific ESG data provides a more informative view of what kind of companies are being compared and is far better than a simple financial analysis can ever be. Thus, what is needed for the investor is to have a minimum set of standardized, and thereby comparable, ESG data indicators that can be used in an efficient overall initial analysis, to sort out which companies to subject to a deep-dive analysis. As long as the research is still waiting for better and more comparable reports, and therefore has not yet defined whether, and potentially what, the value impact is from, for instance, using more or less water per produced unit, lack of diversity in the board of directors, or being better at securing safety for the employees doing the production, then it is up to the investor to decide which indicators should be included in the analysis – but it is surely possible in a fairly objective way, as just demonstrated.

> Most SRI investors seek an Alpha which has an impact on a company's ability to create long-term value. It is the Holy Grail to quantify some of these ESG factors and integrate them with the financial analysis in

order to find such a "sustainability Alpha" that provides a competitive advantage over the investors who do not use such [ESG factors].[18]

Notes

1   Interview with State Authorized Auditor Birgitte Mogensen, former PWC Partner, CSR – now owner of Board Management.
2   Elkington (1997).
3   Page 8 in: http://www.sabmiller.com/files/reports/2012_SD_report.pdf
4   IIRC (2013).
5   IAS 7 (2009).
6   According to IIRC (2013), section 4.19.
7   Hubbard (2009).
8   Kaplan & Norton (1992, 1996).
9   Phillips & Phillips (2011).
10   http://about.puma.com/puma-and-ppr-home-announce-first-results-of-unprecedented-environmental-profit-loss-account/
11   Other things being equal, many PUMA producers may not only have PUMA as a customer, and these are therefore not included in the equation – but obviously PUMA had to choose where to draw the line. This illustrates perfectly why it is so hard to work beyond scope 1 and 2, and at the same time be able to declare anything about completeness.
12   http://about.puma.com/puma-completes-first-environmental-profit-and-loss-account-which-values-impacts-at-e-145-million/
13   Naturally, there is something unattractive and very sensitive about calculating the value of a life or an injury. But to have an impact on investors, we need to evaluate how companies ensure – or not – that their employees and subcontractors do not get hurt. Therefore, the cost in monetary units of having someone injured on a given production must be calculated. Such a calculation could also involve costs as loss of future contracts, if customers are aware of these conditions.
14   See for instance Adams and Ferreira (2009).
15   See also CDP (2012) – comprising primarily data from 2011.
16   To provide discretion, the company names are anonymous.
17   Investors also look at other financial KPIs, but this is the overall primary key used to sort out potential targets.
18   Interview with Dr Helena Barton, Partner, Deloitte Sustainability and (from 2014) Chairman, GRI's Stakeholder Council.

9
CONCLUSION

This book has shown that CSR reporting has implications for stock prices. It is therefore important that the reported CSR data are in such a condition that they can be applied by investors in their analyses. This means that CSR data must be quantitative, reliable, accessible, and not least, comparable. This book demonstrates how companies can ensure their CSR reporting has data of this quality, which can then be included by investors in their analyses. The book also shows how the auditor can help the investor believe that the quality claimed for the data has been verified.

However, is CSR reporting not just a fad, as some claim?[1] Most people interviewed for this book agree that the CSR phenomenon has enough substance to survive the hype – but perhaps in a different form:

> Yes, but it will morph from where it began to something more integrated in standard reporting and hopefully with more reliable/comparable data so that the message companies are trying to get across is indeed meaningful…CSR reporting began mostly as a PR exercise, there is now, however, a very visible trend towards focusing on financial risks, which stem from poor management of ESG issues. This change of focus along with pressure on PRI signatories to show they comply with the principle of integrating ESG factors into investment decisions means that there is a demand for well-structured and data-focused CSR reporting within the investment community.[2]

> Like financial reporting, if CSR reveals previously unknown information it could affect a company in these two ways (red: the demand for shares (and therefore prices) and revenues of a company (and therefore cash flows))…As long as reporting lets investors be the judge I think CSR has a role…[3]

This book has tried to show some of the new paths that an investor could follow to get the most out of the non-financial information that is to be found in CSR reports – paths that on some stretches still need significantly better CSR reporting from companies, as well as extensive new research.

Good luck to all.

Notes

1   See for instance Kristensen (2012).
2   Interview with Kajetan Czyz, Analyst, Governance and Sustainable Investment, in an established asset management company.
3   Interview with Alan Teixeira, Senior Director, IASB.

APPENDIX A
DEFINITION OF CSR AND OTHER
ABBREVIATIONS

CSR = Corporate Social Responsibility

Some companies call their CSR reporting "sustainability reporting", or simply CR[1] or SR, because they understand CSR as a subset of reporting, addressing only the social part of the umbrella concept of sustainability, which also includes other issues, i.e. the environment. For a number of years some companies have had a so-called Health, Safety, and Environment (HSE) or Quality, Health, Safety, and Environment (QHSE) department for making environmental reports, safety reports, etc., to the authorities and thus use this term in their reports.

In this book, CSR is used as a concept in the broadest sense, not least because CSR is the term that most non-CSR experts know. If finance and CSR experts are to have a common vocabulary, we could just decide once and for all that CSR is the abbreviation for Corporate Sustainable Responsibility – then CSR will cover the entire umbrella.

Other abbreviations and acronyms

AA = AccountAbility
ACCA = Association of Chartered Certified Accountants
BSC = Balanced Scorecard
BSR = Business for Social Responsibility
CDP = Carbon Disclosure Project
CDSB = Climate Disclosure Standards Board
CEO = Chief Executive Officer
Ceres = Coalition for Environmentally Responsible Economies
CICA = Canadian Institute of Chartered Accountants
COSO = Committee of Sponsoring Organisations
CO_2e = CO_2 equivalents
COP = Communication on Progress

Defra = Department for Environment, Food and Rural Affairs (UK)

DFVA = Deutsche Vereinigung für Finanzanalyse und Asset

E-P&L = Environmental Profit & Loss Account

EBIT = Earnings Before Interest and Taxes

EBITDA = Earnings Before Interest, Taxes, Depreciation and Amortization

EFFAS = European Federation of Financial Analysts Societies

Eurosif = European Sustainable Investment Forum

ERP = Enterprise Resource Planning (typical abbreviation for the accounting system in most large companies)

ESG = Environmental, Social and corporate Governance

FASB = Financial Accounting Standards Board (US GAAP)

FTE = Full-Time Equivalent (sometimes also translated as Full-Time Employee)

FTSE = *Financial Times* and the London Stock Exchange (UK stock index)

GAAP = Generally Accepted Accounting Principles

GHG = Greenhouse Gas

GRI = Global Reporting Initiative

GWP = Global Warming Potential

HC = Headcount

HFC = Hydrofluorocarbon

IAS = International Accounting Standards

IAASB = International Auditing and Assurance Standards Board

IASB = International Accounting Standards Board

ICRM = Internal Control and Risk Management

IFAC = International Federation of Accountants

IFRIC = International Financial Reporting Interpretations Committee

IFRS = International Financial Reporting Standards

IIRC = International Integrated Reporting Council

ILO = International Labour Organization

IPCC = Intergovernmental Panel on Climate Change

ISA = International Standards on Auditing

ISAE = International Standard on Assurance Engagements

ISEA = Institute of Social and Ethical AccountAbility

ISO = International Organization for Standardization

JO = Joint Operation

JV = Joint Venture

KLD = Kinder Lyderberg Domini Research & Analytics

KPI = Key Performance Indicator

LMS = Learning Management Systems

LTI = Lost Time Injuries

LTIF = Lost Time Injuries Frequency
M&A = Mergers & Acquisitions
OECD = Organisation for Economic Cooperation and Development
P/CO_2e = Price CO_2e
P/CSR = Price CSR
P/E = Price Earnings
PFC = Perfluorocarbon
PIIF = Principles for Investors in Inclusive Finance
P/Pollution = Price Pollution
PRI = Principles for Responsible Investments
PRTR = Pollutant Release and Transfer Register
RI = Responsible Investment
RICC = Risk & Control Compliance
ROIC = Return on Invested Capital
ROP = Return on Pollution
SASB = Sustainability Accounting Standards Board
SBSC = Sustainable Balanced Scorecard
SME = Small and Medium Enterprises
SOP = Standard Operating Procedure
S&P 500 = Standard & Poor's 500
SRI = Socially Responsible Investing
TBL = Triple Bottom Line
UNEP = United Nations Environment Programme
UNGC = United Nations Global Compact
UNPRI = United Nations-supported Principles for Responsible Investment
WRI = World Resources Institution
XBRL = eXtensible Business Reporting Language

Note

1   "CSR/CR/SD is often used interchangeably. CSR is increasingly being seen as closer to the philanthropic community programmes than core business. Ideally they are aligned of course." (Interview with Dave Knight, TwoTomorrows.)

APPFNDIX B
PEOPLE INTERVIEWED FOR THIS BOOK

In connection with the writing of this book, a number of interviews were undertaken. Some were face-to-face and others via correspondence. The following interviewees have contributed and have agreed that their names and positions may be referenced here:

- Dr Helena Barton, Partner, Deloitte Sustainability, and (from 2014), Chairman, Global Reporting Initiative's (GRI) Stakeholder Council
- Kajetan Czyz, Analyst, Governance and Sustainable Investment, in an established international asset management company (company not involved in the interview)
- Lois Guthrie, Executive Director, Climate Disclosure Standards Board (CDSB) and former Technical Director of the International Integrated Reporting Council (IIRC)
- Gordon Hewitt, Sustainability Advisor, Association of Chartered Certified Accountants (ACCA)
- Dr Nancy Kamp-Roelands, when interviewed Executive Director, Ernst & Young, Corporate Responsibility, the Netherlands and Belgium – now Deputy Director of the International Auditing and Assurance Standards Board (IAASB)
- Dave Knight, when interviewed Sustainability Services Director, Two Tomorrows – now DNV Two Tomorrows
- Birgitte Mogensen, when interviewed PWC Partner, CSR – now owner of Board Management
- Charles O'Malley, when interviewed Head of Europe, AccountAbility – now partner at Reos Partners
- François Passant, Executive Director, European Sustainable Investment Forum (Eurosif)
- Alan Teixeira, Senior Director, Technical Activities, International Accounting Standards Board (IASB).

Some of the interviews were undertaken in the autumn of 2012 and some in 2013.

APPENDIX C
COMPANY OVERVIEW

The 50 companies included in the analysis referred to throughout the book are listed in the International Forbes Fortune 2000 overview of the world's largest listed companies, based on 2012 figures. The 50 largest companies were chosen for the analysis and the details are as shown in Table C.1.

The analysis was conducted in the summer and autumn of 2013 based on the most recent CSR reporting made available by the companies on their websites, typically their 2012 reports. The reports included can either be integrated/combined with the financial report, or standalone CSR reports, or may simply comprise internet-based information. The companies' headquarters are situated in all inhabited continents apart from Africa, although most of the companies have subsidiaries in Africa (Figure C.1).

The companies are quite diversified industry-wise and thus the results are considered to be generic.

Note

1   http://www.forbes.com/global2000/list/

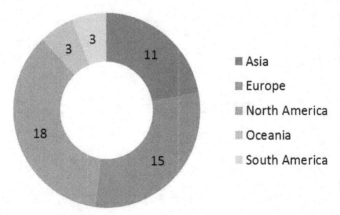

FIGURE C.1   Geographical split of 50 largest listed companies' headquarters

TABLE C.1 The 50 largest listed companies 2012, according to Forbes Fortune 2000[a]

Financial ranking	Company name	Headquarters	Industry	Sales	Profits	Assets	Market value
8	Agricultural Bank of China	China	Banking	103	23	2,124.2	150.8
25	Allianz	Germany	Insurance	140.3	6.8	915.8	66.4
15	Apple	United States	Computer hardware	164.7	41.7	196.1	416.6
24	AT&T	United States	Telecom services	127.4	7.3	272.3	200.1
39	AXA Group	France	Insurance	147.5	5.3	1,005.4	45.3
45	Banco Bradesco	Brazil	Banking	78.3	5.6	417.5	71.6
43	Banco Santander	Spain	Banking	108.8	2.9	1,647.8	82.1
28	Bank of America	United States	Banking	100.1	4.2	2,210	135.5
11	Bank of China	China	Banking	98.1	22.1	2,033.8	131.7
9	Berkshire Hathaway	United States	Investment Services	162.5	14.8	427.5	252.8
44	BHP Billiton	Australia	Materials	72.2	15.4	129.3	184.7
22	BNP Paribas	France	Banking	126.2	8.6	2,504.2	71.3
18	BP	United Kingdom	Oil & Gas	370.9	11.6	301	130.4
13	Chevron	United States	Oil & Gas	222.6	26.2	233	232.5
2	China Construction Bank	China	Banking	113.1	30.6	2,241	202
29	China Mobile	Hong Kong – China	Telecom services	88.8	20.5	168.7	213.8
19	Citigroup	United States	Banking	90.7	7.5	1,864.7	143.6
40	Commonwealth Bank	Australia	Banking	47.8	7.3	735.2	117.5
36	Daimler	Germany	Consumer durables	150.8	8	211.9	64.1
30	ENI	Italy	Oil & Gas	163.7	10	185.2	86.3

(Continued)

TABLE C.1 (Continued)

Financial ranking	Company name	Headquarters	Industry	Sales	Profits	Assets	Market value
5	Exxon Mobil	United States	Oil & Gas	420.7	44.9	333.8	400.4
17	Gazprom	Russia	Oil & Gas	144	40.6	339.3	111.4
4	General Electric	United States	Conglomerate	147.4	13.6	685.3	243.7
49	Goldman Sachs Group	United States	Investment services	41.7	7.5	938.6	74.5
6	HSBC Holdings	United Kingdom	Banking	104.9	14.3	2,684.1	201.3
34	IBM	United States	Software & Services	104.5	16.6	119.2	239.5
1	ICBC	China	Banking	134.8	37.8	2,813.5	237.3
42	Itaú Unibanco Holding	Brazil	Banking	70.5	6.2	453.6	82
46	Johnson & Johnson	United States	Drugs & Biotechnology	67.2	10.9	121.3	221.4
3	JPMorgan Chase	United States	Banking	108.2	21.3	2,359.1	191.4
41	Microsoft	United States	Software & Services	72.9	15.5	128.7	234.8
27	Mitsubishi UFJ Financial	Japan	Banking	59	11.9	2,653.1	85.7
32	Nestlé	Switzerland	Food, Drink, & Tobacco	100.6	11.6	134.7	233.5
46	Nippon Telegraph & Tel	Japan	Telecom services	126.9	5.6	226	58.2
20	Petrobras	Brazil	Oil & Gas	144.1	11	331.6	120.7
9	PetroChina	China	Oil & Gas	308.9	18.3	347.8	261.2
37	Pfizer	United States	Drugs & Biotechnology	59	14.6	185.8	201.4

(Continued)

TABLE C.1 (Continued)

Financial ranking	Company name	Headquarters	Industry	Sales	Profits	Assets	Market value
35	Procter & Gamble	United States	Household & Personal Products	83.3	12.9	139.9	208.5
50	Royal Bank of Canada	Canada	Banking	38.3	7.7	838.5	87.2
7	Royal Dutch Shell	Netherlands	Oil & Gas	467.2	26.6	360.3	213.1
20	Samsung Electronics	South Korea	Semiconductors	187.8	21.7	196.3	174.4
26	Sinopec–China Petroleum	China	Oil & Gas	411.7	10.1	200	106.9
38	Statoil	Norway	Oil & Gas	126.8	12.4	140.2	78.1
23	Total	France	Oil & Gas	240.5	14.1	224.1	115.5
31	Toyota Motor	Japan	Consumer durables	224.5	3.4	371.3	167.2
33	Vodafone	United Kingdom	Telecom services	74.4	11.1	219.9	135.7
14	Volkswagen Group	Germany	Consumer durables	254	28.6	408.2	94.4
15	Wal-Mart Stores	United States	Retailing	469.2	17	203.1	242.5
12	Wells Fargo	United States	Banking	91.2	18.9	1,423	201.3
48	Westpac Banking Group	Australia	Banking	43.9	6.2	699.6	98.9

a All data in billions of US dollars

APPENDIX D
XBRL

XBRL is short for eXtensible Business Reporting Language, which is a technical standard for structured digital reporting of data in a uniform format. XBRL is not an independent accounting standard but it can be used as an extension to various financial and non-financial reporting standards (IFRS, local statutory accounts, GRI, CDSB, etc.). It is also expected that XBRL reporting will be an important reporting form for banks, stock exchanges, institutional investors, trade associations, tax authorities, statistical authorities, and other authorities, because the reporting form means that organizations no longer need to retype the data into their databases; they can simply load the files into the databases. This means less work and fewer typing errors.

The elements that can be included in digital reporting are determined in a so-called taxonomy, which acts as a kind of table of contents or a template. Pairing up the report with the taxonomy is called "tagging". In many countries, there are also requirements for reporting text notes and statements of financial accounts and these must be CLOB (Character Large OBjects) marked,[1] which means that you tag a large character field as one unit. When you have tagged all of the reporting against a given taxonomy, instead of printing the report, you prepare an XBRL file, a so-called XBRL instance, which others can download and read, if they know the taxonomy.

In some countries, is it permissible to use the variant of XBRL called iXBRL (Inline XBRL), making it possible to read the instance with human eyes, as it is presented in HTML with embedded XBRL. A common XBRL instance looks like programming code, and is not directly readable. For this reason, but also for the sake of being able to verify the correctness of the instance, it is recommended that companies use iXBRL.

XBRL has been used for some years in many countries, but mainly for financial and tax information – in many countries it is in fact mandatory to use XBRL when reporting to authorities. But if the taxonomies for CSR reporting are to be used more widely, which will enable the CSR indicators to be in a form that allows the investors and analysts to obtain data in file format for immediate further processing of investor analyses, instead of having to read 80 pages with a little data here and there, it should also be easy for the companies to use the taxonomy and tag the report. This requires standardization form-wise (see Appendix G), just as there now are standards for setting up income statements, balance sheets, cash flow, etc. Thus, XBRL CSR reporting has only recently been made possible with the GRI and CDSB, but is not really widely used – yet. The great thing about XBRL, as the name "eXtensible" indicates, is that the individual taxonomy is not closed. Each taxonomy provides a framework for the basic reporting; but, if a company wants to add more details, it can do so. It dovetails nicely with the idea in this book that there should be minimum requirements for what is reported on CSR, which can be extended by the company, if the company has some specific topics/data, it would like to report further on.

Note

1   CLOB tagging most often means that data are not immediately searchable in a database. For the investor CLOB tagging is therefore close to useless.

APPENDIX E
CONVERSION STANDARDS FOR ENERGY, VOLUME, WEIGHT, AND MASS

Common unit abbreviations:

kilo (k) = 1,000 or 10^3
mega (M) = 1,000,000 or 10^6
giga (G) = 1,000,000,000 or 10^9
tera (T) = 1,000,000,000,000 or 10^{12}
peta (P) = 1,000,000,000,000,000 or 10^{15}

TABLE E.1 Energy conversion standards

	Gigajoule (GJ)	Kilowatt-hour (kWh)	Therm	Tonne oil equivalent (toe)	Kilocalorie (kCal)
Gigajoule (GJ)[a]	1	277.78	9.47817	0.02388	238,903
Kilowatt-hour (kWh)	0.0036	1	0.03412	0.00009	860.05
Therm	0.10551	29.307	1	0.00252	25,206
Tonne oil equivalent (toe)	41.868	11,630	396.83	1	10,002,389
Kilocalorie (kCal)	0.000004186	0.0011627	0.000039674	0.0000001	1

a As an example of using the tables, this should be read as follows: 1 gigajoule (GJ) is equivalent to 277.78 kilowatt hours (kWh)

TABLE E.2 Volume conversion standards

	Litres (L)	Cubic metres (m³)	Cubic feet (cu ft)	Imperial gallon	US gallon	Barrel – US, petroleum (bbl)
Litres, L	1	0.001	0.03531	0.21997	0.26417	0.0062898
Cubic metres (m³)	1,000	1	35.315	219.97	264.17	6.2898
Cubic feet (cu ft)	28.317	0.02832	1	6.2288	7.48052	0.17811
Imperial gallon	4.5461	0.00455	0.16054	1	1.20095	0.028594
US gallon	3.7854	0.0037854	0.13368	0.83267	1	0.02381
Barrel – US, petroleum (bbl)	158.99	0.15899	5.6146	34.972	42	1

TABLE E.3 Weight and mass conversion standards

	Kilogram (kg)	Tonne (t) (metric tonne)	Ton (UK, long ton)	Ton (US, short ton)	Pound (lb)
Kilogram (kg)	1	0.001	0.00098	0.0011	2.20462
Tonne (t) (metric tonne)	1,000	1	0.98421	1.10231	2,204.62
Ton (UK, long ton)	1,016.04642	1.01605	1	1.12	2,240
Ton (US, short ton)	907.18	0.90718	0.89286	1	2,000
Pound (lb)	0.45359	0.00045359	0.00044643	0.0005	1

Source: 2012 Guidelines to Defra/DECC's GHG *Conversion Factors for Company Reporting*. Produced by AEA for the Department of Energy and Climate Change (DECC) and the Department for Environment, Food and Rural Affairs (Defra). https://www.gov.uk/government/uploads/system/uploads/attachment_data/file/69554/pb13773-ghg-conversion-factors-2012.pdf

APPENDIX F
FORMULAS

Environmental data

CO_2 equivalents (CO_2e)

The following formulas can be used in the calculation of CO_2e. Some of the formulas represent certain simplifications in the assumptions underlying their use. If the company wishes to obtain a more accurate value, it can choose to measure GHGs directly, or use more fine-grained models, which can be found on the internet. However, for most companies the formulas given below will do. The gases in the Kyoto protocol, such as CO_2, CH_4, N_2O, SF_6, etc., whose measurements are based on combustion, are calculated using the same formula, just with different converters; these differ with respect to the type of fuel combusted and thus fuel types also need to be calculated separately (in the examples, 't' = metric tonnes throughout).
Example:

$$CH_4 \text{ (t)} = \Sigma \text{ [combusted fuel type (t)} \times CH_4 \text{ conversion factor per fuel type]}_{\text{per fuel type}}$$

The above CO_2e must be calculated separately for scope 1 and scope 2. Subsequently, these are summed to provide an overall GHG figure.[1]

$$GHG \text{ (t)} = CO_2e \text{ (t)} = CO_2 \text{ t} + (25 \times CH_4 \text{ t}) + (298 \times N_2O \text{ t}) + (22,800 \times SF_6 \text{ t}) + (GWP \text{ factor} \times HFC \text{ t}) + (GWP \text{ factor} \times PFC \text{ t})$$

CO_2e for HFCs and PFCs are calculated as other GHGs are according to combustion, but GWP factors depend on the fuels used in the company. The specific GWPs can be found through the Intergovernmental Panel on Climate Change (IPCC) homepage.[2] The IPCC has now published the fourth generation of analyses, which are from 2007. In most companies, HFC and PFC emissions are usually quite minimal.

Energy

Energy (GJ) = Σ(combusted fuel type (t) × power factor per fuel type)$_{\text{per fuel type}}$ + (used electricity (including renewable energy)(MWh) × 3.6) + (used district heating including renewable sources of heat) (GJ)

Social data

Full-Time Equivalents (FTE)

FTE = Σ [(total number of compensated hours)/(norm hours for a full-time employee)]$_{\text{per country}}$

The standard time varies around the world depending on working hours, holiday entitlements and holidays, etc. It is therefore important that the standard time – and thereby the FTEs – are calculated locally and then consolidated to provide corporate figures according to regular financial consolidation rules. According to the OECD, the average annual norm time is somewhere between 1,400 and 2,200 hours in case you want to sanity-check the link between FTEs versus exposure hours.

Lost Time Injuries (LTI) frequency

LTI frequency = (LTI number × 1,000,000)/exposure hours

Ratios

Pollution

Pollution is measured in the currency unit, which is also used to calculate financial data.

Pollution is measured in accordance with minimum data by summing:

(CO_2e t × CO_2 quota price) + (water consumption × generic water price) + (waste per type × generic waste price per waste type)

It should be noted that pollution data only relate to scopes 1 and 2, i.e. those directly attributable to pollution in the production of the company. Scope 3 is too vague a concept and cannot be compared between companies and should therefore not be included in ratios.

Return on Pollution (ROP)

ROP can be measured as follows:

[(continuing operation profit after tax but before deduction of minority interests)/pollution] × 100

ROP is measured in percent.

CSR factor

CSR factor = pollution + social factor + governance factor

The social factor consists of a monetary recalculation of the value of lack of safety (dead and injured), inequality in the management layer (such as the opportunity cost of not having equality) minus the net positive value of donations including working hours contributed to society for the company.

The governance factor consists of a monetary recalculation of the cost of a lack of an audit committee, high seniority on the board, and/or audit inequality on the board, etc.

There is no valid calculation of either the social factor or the governance factor yet because research lacks valid CSR reports to establish possible standards for these elements and their related opportunity costs. Until such time as there is a valid measurement, companies and investors must settle for pollution figures.

Price CSR (P/CSR)

P/CSR = share price/(CSR-factor/number of shares)

As the CSR factor cannot currently be calculated because the data are still too weak, as a substitute, P/Pollution, with the limitations this implies, will have to do.

Price Pollution (P/ Pollution)

P/Pollution = share price/(pollution/number of shares)

Price CO₂ (P/CO₂)

P/CO$_2$ is the simple version of the two previous ratios with the minimum recalculation, which all companies and investors can undertake immediately, as shown in Chapter 8 "How can investors use CSR in their analysis of stocks?" It works best when compared with the Price Earnings (P/E) value.

$$P/CO_2 = \text{share price}/[(\text{scope 1} + \text{scope 2 } CO_2e)/\text{number of shares}]$$

Notes

1 HFC = hydrofluorocarbons; PFC = perfluorocarbons.
2 http://www.ipcc.ch/publications_and_data/ar4/wg1/en/ch2s2-10-2.html

APPENDIX G
CSR NOTE FORMS

TABLE G.1 Classic CSR note

Standard CSR note – ESG friendly	Unit	Year-4	Year-3	Year-2	Year-1	Year
Environmental data						
CO_2-equivalents scope 1	CO_2e-t					
CO_2-equivalents scope 2	CO_2e-t					
CO_2-equivalents total	CO_2e-t					
CO_2 per quantity	CO_2e-t					
Energy	GJ					
Energy-efficiency	CO_2e-t per GJ					
Drinking water	m^3					
Groundwater	m^3					
Surface water	m^3					
Seawater	m^3					
Collected rainwater	m^3					
Gross water consumption total	m^3					
Purified and released water	m^3					
Net water consumption total	m^3					
Water consumption per quantity	m^3					
Waste, recycling	t					
Waste, combustion	t					
Waste, landfill	t					
Waste, special treatment	t					
Waste total	t					
Waste per quantity	t					

(Continued)

TABLE G.1 (Continued)

Standard CSR not ESG friendly	Unit	Year 4	Year 3	Year 2	Year 1	Year
Social data						
Corporate Presidents and Vice Presidents (women %)	FTEs (%)					
Directors (women %)	FTEs (%)					
Managers (women %)	FTEs (%)					
Other employees (women %)	FTEs (%)					
Total employees (women %)	FTEs (%)					
Accidents, own employees	LTIs (LTIF)					
Accidents, contract workers	LTIs (LTIF)					
Accidents, subcontractors	LTIs					
Accidents, third parties	LTIs					
Accidents total	LTIs					
Fatalities, own employees	No.					
Fatalities, contract workers	No.					
Fatalities, subcontractors	No.					
Fatalities, third parties	No.					
Fatalities total	No.					
External training hours per employee	Hours					
Internal training hours per employee	Hours					
Total training hours per employee	Hours					
Voluntary work for community	Hours					
Donations, benevolent purposes	Monetary unit					
Donations, political parties	Monetary unit					
Donations, other associations	Monetary unit					
Donations, anonymous grants for activities or acquisitions	Monetary unit					
Donations total	Monetary unit					

(Continued)

TABLE G.1 (Continued)

Standard CSR note – ESG friendly	Unit	Year-4	Year-3	Year-2	Year-1	Year
Governance data						
Size of the board including employee representatives (women %)	No. (%)					
Size of the board excluding employee representatives (women %)	No. (%)					
Number of board meetings	No.					
Average duration of service on the board including employee representatives	Years					
Average duration of service on the board excluding employee representatives	Years					
Number of audit committee meetings	No.					
Duration of the financial auditor relationship with the company	Years					
Duration of the non-financial auditor/reviewer relationship with the company	Years					
Ratios						
P/CO_2	Monetary unit					
Pollution	Monetary unit					
Return on Pollution	%					
P/Pollution	Monetary unit					
And when better data quality and reports have made way for extensive research, these ratios should also be included:						
CSR factor	Monetary unit					
P/CSR	Monetary unit					

TABLE G.2 Integrated note[a]

Integrated note	Unit	Year 4	Year 3	Year 2	Year 1	Year
Input data						
Total assets, primo	Monetary unit					
Equity, primo	Monetary unit					
Total liabilities, primo	Monetary unit					
Share price, primo	Monetary unit					
Number of shares, primo	No.					
Capital injections	Monetary unit					
Loans granted from others	Monetary unit					
Customer payments	Monetary unit					
Divestitures	Monetary unit					
Net financial income	Monetary unit					
Use of oil	t					
Use of gas	t					
Use of diesel	t					
Use of gasoline	t					
Use of kerosene	t					
Use of coal	t					
Use of biomass	t					
Use of electricity	GJ					
Use of district heating	GJ					
Drinking water	m^3					
Groundwater	m^3					
Surface water	m^3					
Seawater	m^3					
Collected rainwater	m^3					
Gross water consumption total	m^3					
Purified and released water	m^3					
Net water consumption total	m^3					
Corporate Presidents and Vice Presidents (women %)	FTEs (%)					
Directors (women %)	FTEs (%)					
Managers (women %)	FTEs (%)					
Other employees (women %)	FTEs (%)					
Total employees (women %)	FTEs (%)					

(Continued)

TABLE G.2 (Continued)

Integrated note	Unit	Year-4	Year-3	Year-2	Year-1	Year
External training hours per employee	Hours					
Internal training hours per employee	Hours					
Total training hours per employee	Hours					
Size of the board including employee representatives (women %)	No. (%)					
Size of the board excluding employee representatives (women %)	No. (%)					
Number of board meetings	No.					
Average duration of service on the board including employee representatives	Years					
Average duration of service on the board excluding employee representatives	Years					
Number of audit committee meetings	No.					
Duration of the financial auditor relationship with the company	Years					
Duration of the non-financial auditor/ reviewer relationship with the company	Years					

Output data

Integrated note	Unit	Year-4	Year-3	Year-2	Year-1	Year
Quantities of production Quantitative unit						
CO_2-equivalents scope 1	CO_2e-t					
CO_2-equivalents scope 2	CO_2e-t					
CO_2-equivalents total	CO_2e-t					
CO_2 per quantity	CO_2e-t					

(Continued)

TABLE G.2 (Continued)

Integrated note	Unit	Year 4	Year 3	Year 2	Year 1	Year
Water consumption per quantity	m³					
Waste, recycling	t					
Waste, combustion	t					
Waste, landfill	t					
Waste, special treatment	t					
Waste total	t					
Waste per quantity	t					
Outcome and impact data						
Net result before minorities	Monetary unit					
Total assets, ultimo	Monetary unit					
Equity, ultimo	Monetary unit					
Total liabilities, ultimo	Monetary unit					
Share price, ultimo	Monetary unit					
Number of shares, ultimo	No.					
Salaries paid	Monetary unit					
Taxes paid	Monetary unit					
Vendor payments	Monetary unit					
Dividends paid	Monetary unit					
Repaid loans or loans granted to others	Monetary unit					
Investments	Monetary unit					
Donations, benevolent purposes	Monetary unit					
Donations, political parties	Monetary unit					
Donations, other associations	Monetary unit					
Donations, anonymous grants for activities or acquisitions	Monetary unit					
Donations total	Monetary unit					
Energy	GJ					
Energy efficiency	CO_2e-t per GJ					
Accidents, own employees	LTIs (LTIF)					
Accidents, contract workers	LTIs (LTIF)					

(Continued)

TABLE G.2 (Continued)

Integrated note	Unit	Year-4	Year-3	Year-2	Year-1	Year
Accidents, subcontractors	LTIs					
Accidents, third parties	LTIs					
Accidents total	LTIs					
Fatalities, own employees	No.					
Fatalities, contract workers	No.					
Fatalities, subcontractors	No.					
Fatalities, third parties	No.					
Fatalities total	No.					
Voluntary work for community	Hours					
P/CO$_2$	Monetary unit					
Pollution	Monetary unit					
Return on Pollution	%					
P/Pollution	Monetary unit					

And when better data quality and reports have made way for extensive research, these ratios should also be included:

CSR factor	Monetary unit					
P/CSR	Monetary unit					

a Inspired by IIRC (2013), sections 4.14–4.20

REFERENCES[1]

ACCA (2008). *Social and Environmental Narrative Reporting – Analysts' Perceptions.* ACCA Research report No. 104. Prepared by Campbell, D. & Slack, R. Available online at www.accaglobal.com/content/dam/acca/global/PDF-technical/ sustainability-reporting/tech_tp_sen.pdf (last accessed 22 February 2014).

ACCA & Eurosif (2013). *What Do Investors Expect from Non-financial Reporting?* Available online at www.accaglobal.com/content/dam/acca/global/PDF-technical/ sustainability-reporting/tech-tp-wdir.pdf

AccountAbility (2006). *Guidance Note on the Principles of Materiality, Completeness and Responsiveness as They Relate to the AA1000 Assurance Standard.* Available online at www.accountability.org/images/content/1/8/189/AA1000%20Guidance%20 Note%20-%20Low%20Res.pdf (last accessed 25 February 2014).

Adams, R. B. & Ferreira, D. (2009). Women in the Boardroom and Their Impact on Governance and Performance. *Journal of Financial Economics, 94*, 291–309.

Ali, I., Rehman, K. U., Ali, S., I., Yousaf, J. & Zia, M. (2010). Corporate Social Responsibility Influences Employee Commitment and Organizational Performance. *African Journal of Business Management, 4*(12), 2796–2801. Available online at http://nachhaltig-sein.info/wp-content/uploads/2012/12/Ali-et-al_ CSR-Influences-employee-commitment-and-organizational-performance.pdf (last accessed 9 March 2014).

Barnea, A. & Rubin, A. (2010). Corporate Social Responsibility as a Conflict Between Shareholders. *Journal of Business Ethics, 97*, 71–86.

Bernstein, A. (2009). *Quantifying Labor and Human Rights Portfolio Risk, Capital Matters No. 4, June 2009.* Occasional Paper Series, Harvard Law School. Available online at www.law.harvard.edu/programs/lwp/pensions/publications/occpapers/ occasionalpapers4.pdf

BertelsmannStiftung (2006). *Who Is Who in Corporate Social Responsibility Rating? A Survey of Internationally Established Rating Systems that Measure Corporate Responsibility.* Prepared by Schäfer, H., Beer, J., Zenker, J. & Fernandes, P. (University of Stuttgart), published by the Bertelsmann Foundation. Available online at www. bertelsmann-stiftung.de/cps/rde/xbcr/SID-3B123554-CF0F61D6/bst_engl/ Who_is_who%20in_CSR-Rating_.pdf

Brammer, S., Brooks, C. & Pavelin, S. (2006). Corporate Social Performance and Stock Returns: UK Evidence from Disaggregate Measures. *Financial Management*, 35(3), 97–116.

CDP (2012). *CDP S&P 500 Climate Change Report 2012 – Accelerating Progress Toward a Lower-Carbon Future*. Available online at www.cdp.net/cdpresults/cdp-sp500-2012.pdf

CDSB (2012). *Climate Change Reporting Framework* (ed. 1.1, October 2012). Available online at www.cdsb.net/sites/cdsbnet/files/cdsbframework_v1-1.pdf

Chatterji, A. & Levine, D. (2005). *Breaking Down the Wall of Codes: Evaluating Non-Financial Performance Measurement*. Working Paper Series, Center for Responsible Business, UC Berkeley. Published in 2006 in *California Management Review*, 48(2). Available online at http://faculty.haas.berkeley.edu/levine/papers/Chatterji&%20Levine%20Wall%20of%20Codes%20CMR.pdf (last accessed 9 March 2014).

CICA (2010). *Environmental, Social and Governance (ESG) Issues in Institutional Investor Decision Making*. Available online at www.cica.ca/publications/list-of-publications/manual/item41881.pdf

Collings, S. (2011). *Interpretation and Application of International Standards of Auditing*. John Wiley & Sons Ltd, West Sussex.

Defra (2013). *Environmental Reporting Guidelines: Including Mandatory Greenhouse Gas Emissions Reporting Guidance* (June 2013). Available online at www.gov.uk/government/uploads/system/uploads/attachment_data/file/206392/pb13944-env-reporting-guidance.pdf

Dhaliwal, D.S., Li, O. Z., Tsang, A. & Yang, Y. G. (2011). Voluntary Nonfinancial Disclosure and the Cost of Equity Capital: The Initiation of Corporate Social Responsibility Reporting. *The Accounting Review*, 86(1), 59–100.

Eccles, E.G. & Krzus, M.P. (2010). *One Report – Integrated Reporting for a Sustainable Strategy*. John Wiley & Sons Inc., Hoboken, NJ.

EFFAS and DFVA (2010). *KPIs for ESG – A Guideline for the Integration of ESG into the Financial Analysis and Corporate Valuation*. Available online at www.effas-esg.com/wp-content/uploads/2011/07/KPIs_for_ESG_3_0_Final.pdf

Elkington, J. (1997). *Cannibals with Forks – The Triple Bottom Line of 21st Century Business*. Capstone Publishing Ltd, Oxford.

Ferreira, A., Moulang, C. & Hendro, B. (2010). Environmental Management Accounting and Innovation: An Exploratory Analysis. *Accounting, Auditing & Accountability Journal*, 23(7), 920–948.

Flammer, C. (2012) Corporate Social Responsibility and Shareholder Reaction: The Environmental Awareness of Investors. *Academy of Management Journal*, published before print July 2012 (published June 1, 2013, 56(3), 758–781).

Füchsel, K., Gath, P., Langsted, L.B. & Skovby, J. (2005). *Revisor – regulering & rapportering*. Forlaget Thomson, København.

Goldman Sachs (2009). *GS SUSTAIN: Challenges in ESG Disclosure and Consistency* (October 2009). Available online at www.sseinitiative.org/files/GS_SUSTAIN_Challenges_in_ESG_disclosure_and_consistency.pdf

GRI (2013). *G4 Sustainability Reporting Guidelines, Reporting Principles and Standard Disclosures*. Available online at www.globalreporting.org/resourcelibrary/GRIG4-Part1-Reporting-Principles-and-Standard-Disclosures.pdf

Hamid, U. & Johner, O. (2010). The United Nations Global Compact Communication on Progress Policy: Origins, Trends and Challenges. In Rasche, A. & Kell, G. (Eds), *The United Nations Global Compact – Achievements, Trends and Challenges*. Cambridge University Press.

Hawken, P. (2004). *Social Responsible Investing – How the SRI Industry Has Failed to Respond to People Who Want to Invest with Conscience and What Can Be Done to Change It*. Natural Capital Institute, California. Available online at www.naturalcapital.org/docs/SRI%20Report%2010-04_word.pdf

Hubbard, G. (2009). Measuring Organizational Performance: Beyond the Triple Bottom Line. *Business Strategy and the Environment*, *18*(3), 177–191. Available online at http://onlinelibrary.wiley.com/doi/10.1002/bse.564/pdf

Hull, C.E. & Rothenberg, S. (2008). Firm Performance: The Interactions of Corporate Social Performance with Innovation and Industry Differentiation. *Strategic Management Journal*, *29*, 781–789.

IAASB (2011). *ISAE 3000 (Revised), Assurance Engagements Other than Audits or Reviews of Historical Financial Information*. Available online at www.ifac.org/sites/default/files/publications/exposure-drafts/IAASB_ISAE_3000_ED.pdf

Iansen-Rogers, J. & Oelschlaegel, J. (2005). *Assurance Standards Briefing – AA1000 Standard & ISAE3000*. KPMG & Accountability, London.

IAS 7 (2009). *Statement of Cash Flow (effective from 2010)*. Available online at www.iasplus.com/en/standards/ias/ias7

IAS 17 (2009). *Leases (effective from 2010)*. Available online at www.iasplus.com/en/standards/ias/ias17

IASB (2013). *Heads Up — Boards review feedback on the revised leases exposure draft*. Available online at www.iasplus.com/en/publications/us/heads-up/2013/leases-feedback

IFRIC 4 (2004). *Determining Whether an Arrangement Contains a Lease (effective from 2006)*. Available online at www.iasplus.com/en/standards/ifric/ifric4

IFRS 8 (2009). *Operating Segments (effective from 2010)*. Available online at www.iasplus.com/en/standards/ifrs/ifrs8

IFRS 10 (2012). *Consolidated Financial Statements (effective from 2013)*. Available online at www.iasplus.com/en/standards/ifrs/ifrs10

IFRS 11 (2012). *Joint Arrangements (effective from 2013)*. Available online at www.iasplus.com/en/standards/ifrs/ifrs11

IIRC (2013). *The international <IR> framework*. Available online at www.theiirc.org/wp-content/uploads/2013/12/13-12-08-THE-INTERNATIONAL-IR-FRAMEWORK-2-1.pdf

ILO (1998). *Fundamental Principles on Rights at Work*. Available online at www.ilo.org/declaration/thedeclaration/textdeclaration/lang--en/index.htm (last accessed 11 March 2014).

Institut RSE Management (2012). *The Grenelle II Act in France: a milestone towards integrated reporting*. Available online at www.capitalinstitute.org/sites/capitalinstitute.

org/files/docs/Institut%20RSE%20The%20grenelle%20II%20Act%20in%20
France%20June%202012.pdf

Ioannou, I. & Serafeim, G. (2011). *The Impact of Corporate Social Responsibility on Investment Recommendations.* Working paper 11-017, Harvard Business School, MA.

Ioannou, I. & Serafeim, G. (2012). *The Consequences of Mandatory Corporate Sustainability Reporting.* Working paper 11-100, Harvard Business School, MA.

ISEA (2011). *AA1000 Series of Standards.* Available online at http://www.accountability.org/standards/

ISO (2010). *ISO 26000.* Available online at http://www.iso.org/iso/home/standards/management-standards/iso26000.htm

Jagd, J.T. (2013). *Investor orienteret CSR-rapportering.* Karnov Group, København.

Jeppesen, C.S. & Madsen, K. (2011). *Analyse af årsregnskabsmeddelelsers nyhedsværdi – et eventstudie på det danske aktiemarked.* Professional master's thesis published by Revifora & Thomson Reuters, cand.merc.aud. København.

Kamp-Roelands, N. (2002). *Towards a Framework for Auditing Environmental Reports.* Doctoral dissertation, Tilburg University, The Netherlands.

Kaplan, R. & Norton, D. (1992). The Balanced Scorecard – Measures that Drive Performance. *Harvard Business Review, 70*(1), 71–79.

Kaplan, R. & Norton, D. (1996). *The Balanced Scorecard – Translating Strategy into Action.* Harvard Business School Press, MA.

Knox, S. & Maklan, S. (2004). Corporate Social Responsibility: Moving Beyond Investment Towards Measuring Outcomes. *European Management Journal, 22*(5), 508–516.

KPMG (2013). *The KPMG Survey of Corporate Responsibility Reporting 2013.* KPMG International.

Kristensen, O. P. (2012, November 14). Kejserens nye CSR-klæder. *Børsen.*

Leipziger, D. (2010). *The Corporate Responsibility Code Book* (revised 2nd ed.). Greenleaf Publishing Limited, Sheffield.

Maguire, M. (2011). *The Future of Corporate Social Responsibility Reporting.* Issues in Brief, No. 19, January 2011. The Frederick S. Pardee Center for the Study of the Longer-Range Future, Boston University, MA.

Margolis, J. D., Elfenbein, H. A. & Walsh, J. P. (2009). *Does It Pay to Be Good … and Does It Matter? A Meta-Analysis of the Relationship Between Corporate Social and Financial Performance, SSR.* Available online at http://ssrn.com/abstract=1866371

Mogensen, B., Christensen, A.M., Pedersen, M.L.H. & Holbech, A. (2011). *Corporate Social Responsibility – en guide for virksomheder og organisationer.* Thomson Reuters Professional, København.

Morris, J. (2012). *The Five W's of France's CSR Reporting Law.* BSR, July 2. Available online at www.bsr.org/reports/The_5_Ws_of_Frances_CSR_Reporting_Law_FINAL.pdf

OECD (1976). *OECD Guidelines for Multinational Enterprises.*

OECD (2004). *OECD Principles of Corporate Governance.* Available online at www.oecd.org/daf/ca/corporategovernanceprinciples/31557724.pdf

OECD (2011) *OECD Guidelines for Multinational Enterprises.* Available online at www.oecd.org/investment/mne/48004323.pdf (last accessed 17 March 2014).

OECD (2013). *Health Data 2013 – Definitions, Sources and Methods* (October 2013). Available online at www.oecd.org/health/healthdata

Orlitzky, M., Schmidt, F.L. & Rynes, S.L. (2003). Corporate Social and Financial Performance: A Meta-analysis. *Organization Studies, 24*(3), 403–441.

Phillips, P.P. & Phillips, J.J. (2011). *The Green Scorecard – Measuring the Return on Investment in Sustainability Initiatives.* Nicholas Brealey Publishing, Boston, MA.

Roepstorff, A. & Serpa, L.B. (2005). *Katalog over CSR-værktøjer.* Erhvervs- og Selskabsstyrelsen. Available online at http://www.eogs.dk/graphics/publikationer/CSR/Katalog-over-CSR-vaerktoejer.pdf (last accessed 9 March 2014).

Samuelsen, M. (2007). Revisionsstandarder RS 500 og RS 501. *INSPI, 37*(5).

Schur, A.-L.T., Reissmann, M. & Rosenstock, M. (2011). *Hvad enhver virksomhed bør vide om CSR, lovgivning, forbrugere og medier.* L&R Business, Egmont, København.

Sullivan, R. (2011). *Valuing Corporate Responsibility – How Do Investors Really Use Corporate Responsibility Information?* Greenleaf Publishing Limited, Sheffield.

UN (1987) *Report of the World Commission on Environment and Development: Our Common Future.* Available online at www.un-documents.net/our-common-future.pdf

UN (2011) *United Nations Guiding Principles on Business and Human Rights.* Available online at www.ohchr.org/Documents/Publications/GuidingPrinciplesBusinessHR_EN.pdf

UNEP, GRI, KPMG and Centre for Corporate Governance in Africa (2013). *Carrots and sticks, Sustainability Reporting Policies Worldwide – Today's Best Practice, Tomorrow's Trends.* Available online at www.globalreporting.org/resourcelibrary/Carrots-and-Sticks.pdf

UNEP & UNGC (2006). *Principles for Responsible Investments.* Available online at www.unpri.org/viewer/?file=files/20060427_press/un-unepfi-gc_press_20060427.pdf

UNPRI, UNEP & UNGC (2011) *Principles for Investors in Inclusive Finance (PIIF).* Available online at http://www.unpri.org/viewer/?file=wp-content/uploads/PrinciplesforInvestorsinInclusiveFinance.pdf

UNPRI, UNEP & UNGC (2012). *Principles for Investors in Inclusive Finance (PIIF).* Available online at www.unpri.org/viewer/?file=files/2012.05.02%20PIIF%20info%20pack.pdf

UNPRI (2013). *PRI Reporting Framework 2013/14 – Overview and Guidance* (October 2013). Available online at www.unpri.org/viewer/?file=wp-content/uploads/2013-14_PRI_RF_overviewandguidance.pdf

Vogel, D. (2006). *The Market for Virtue – The Potential and Limits of Corporate Social Responsibility* (paperback edition). Brookings Institution Press, Washington, DC.

Wang, M., Qiu, C. & Kong, D. (2011). Corporate Social Responsibility, Investor Behaviors, and Stock Market Returns: Evidence from a Natural Experiment in China. *Journal of Business Ethics, 101*(1), 127–141.

WestLB (2008). *ESG Reporting – Aiming to Uncover the True Performance.* Paper presented at the Faire Conference, Paris, 12 June 2008. Available online at www.frenchsif.org/pdf/FAIRE/edition2008/westlb_esg_presentation.pdf

WRI (2001) *The Greenhouse Gas Protocol – A Corporate Accounting and Reporting Standard*. Available online at www.ghgprotocol.org/files/ghgp/public/ghg-protocol-2001.pdf

Yip, R.W.Y. & Young, D. (2012). Does Mandatory IFRS Adoption Improve Information Comparability? *The Accounting Review, 87*(5), 1767–1789.

Note

1   Unless otherwise indicated, all websites were last accessed on 14 January 2014

INDEX

AA 1000 Series *see AccountAbility AA 1000 Series of Standards* (2011)
accessible data 1, 19, 34, 111
accidents 39, 71–2, **130**, **134**
AccountAbility AA 1000 Series of Standards (2003) **12**
AccountAbility AA 1000 Series of Standards (2008) **12**
AccountAbility AA 1000 Series of Standards (2011) **12**, 22–3
accounting: *AA1000 Assurance Standard (AS)* 22; *see also* XBRL International
airmiles 63
Anan, Kofi 14
anti-corruption data omitted in study of 50 largest companies' reports 58
associated companies 57
Association of Chartered Certified Accountants (ACCA) 2, 6
audit committees 50, 76, 83, 90–3, 105, 109
audit trail *24*, 95–6
audits, non-financial *see* ISAE 3000
audits and auditors 9, 23–6, 47–50, 57, 59–60, 62, 69, 76, 78–81, 83, 85, 88, 90

balance sheet 42, 122
Balanced Scorecard (BSC) 103
Barton, Helena 110n18, 116
benchmark 18
Berkshire Hathaway 57–8
biomass 62, **86**, **132**
Bloomberg, basic CSR data requirements of 43
board of directors 57, **70**, 109

boundaries, financial: advantages of parallel data in financial report and CSR report 41–2; consolidation method 41; leasing, effect on reporting 51n11; safety standards reporting 38
boundaries, operational: definition 35; and joint operations 39; leasing, effect on reporting 51n11; problem of completeness 40–2; variations across industries and countries 40
Brundtland Report (1987) **12**
business ethics: data omitted in study of 50 largest companies' reports 58; ISO 26000 (2010) 17; *OECD Guidelines for Multinational Enterprises* 14; UN Global Compact, Ten Principles **16**

Cadbury Schweppes' CSR Report *44–5*
Canadian Institute of Chartered Accountants 42
carbon dioxide (CO_2) 17, 37, 39, *108*, 128
Carbon Disclosure Project (2000) **12**; Global 500 best performing companies analysis 107, **108**, 109
Carbon Disclosure Standards Board (CDSB) *see* CDSB Framework
carbon emissions *see* Greenhouse Gas (GHG) Protocol
Carlsberg 8
cash flow 35–7, 39, 41–2, 67, 85, 101–2, 108, 111, 122

CDSB Framework: reports on greenhouse gas emissions 35; role in suggested mandatory CSR reporting 53
cherry-picking 59, 60, 62
Climate Disclosure Project (CDP) **13**
Climate Disclosure Standards Board (CDSB) **13**
CO_2 equivalents 61, 63, 125
coal 62, **86**, **132**
Coalition for Environmentally Responsible Economies (Ceres) 18
Committee of Sponsoring Organizations (COSO), model for SOX regulations 84
Communication on Progress (COP) 15, 44
community involvement: ISO 26000 (2010) 17; *see also* social data
company data or SRI agency surveys, source of reports 9
comparability 19, 23, 27, 33, 35, 46, 48, 53–4, 58–60, 62
compensation affected by operational boundary decisions 39
competition, *OECD Guidelines for Multinational Enterprises* 14
competitors 5, 8, 60, 66, 102–3
completeness 19, 22, 27, 37, 40–2, 62–3, 73, 81n1, 90–1, 96
comply or explain 15, 21, 46
composting 66
consolidation 35–6, 39–42, 50, 54, 60, 62, 64, 67, 69–70, 77n28, 95–7, 99, 126
consumer issues, ISO 26000 (2010) 17
consumption 50, 80, 86; electricity 85, 97, 98; fuel 62–4; water 55, 64–5, 67, 80, 86, 94, 103–4, 106, 109, 126, **129**, **132**, **134**
control catalogue 84, 88–94
control environment: annual process *84*; local verification 97–8; monitoring 93–4; parallels to financial reporting 82–3
control objective 83–5, 87–8, 90–2
converters 50, 61–4, 77n19, 98, 125
corporate citizens, managers as 6
corporate comparisons 35, 102–3; PUMA (PPR Home) study results 102–3, 105

corporate impact, Global Reporting Initiative (G4) reporting 19
Corporate Social Responsibility (CSR), definition 113, 115n1
corruption **16**, 58
CSR accounting principles 49
CSR data collection with financial data, benefits of 96
CSR employees 42, 96
CSR factor 106–7, 127, **131**, **135**
CSR per share 6, 106
CSR rating 1–2, 5–7, 9, 43
CSR reporting compliance methods, centralized and decentralized 83, 87
CSR reporting, history of **12–13**
CSR reporting, study of 50 largest companies' reports indicators 55
CSR reviewers: *AA1000 Assurance Standard (AS)* 22, 48; *AA1000 Assurance Standard (AS)* compliance 83
Czyz, Karetan 112n2, 116

data, standard, accessible and quantified 42, 54
data collection: boundaries, financial 36; boundaries, operational 35–6; within financial boundaries 35; improvements needed 33; inconsistencies 54; leasing, effect on reporting 37–8; standard, accessible and quantified 34
data discipline 2, 40, 107
data types, documentable and probable 79–81
delivery notes 63, 65, 79
Deloitte **13**
Deutsche Bank 5
diesel 62, **86**, **132**
district heating 63–4, **86**, 98, 126, **132**
documentation 50, 73, 78–80; invoices for employees 69, 73; invoices for materials 62–3, 65; pay slips 79
donations 56, 67, 73–4, 80, **86**, 102, 127, **130**, **134**
Dow Jones 9, 109
duration *see* governance data

Earnings Before Interest, Taxes, Depreciation and Amortisation (EBITDA) 41

earnings per share (EPS) 108
economic argument, capital cost savings
1 6
economy, Global Reporting Initiative
(GRI) level A reporting 20
electricity 18, 63–4, 79, 85, **86**, 94, 97–8,
104, 126, **132**
Elkington, John 101, 103
emissions 29, 37–9, 55, 61, 98, 125; *see
also* greenhouse gas emissions
employees 22, 55–7, 66–74, **86**, 87, 126,
130–5
energy data, risk assessment **86**
Environmental, Social and Corporate
Governance (ESG) performance 10,
43, 55, 58
environmental data: calculation of
pollution cost 106; CO_2 equivalents
scope 1 61–3; CO_2 equivalents
scope 2 63–4; defined 60–1; energy
produced using different fuels 64;
PUMA (PPR Home) study 103–4;
relation to production quantities
66–7; Return on Pollution (ROP)
ratio 105–6; risk assessment **86**;
SBSC data used internally 103; study
of 50 largest companies' reports
indicators 55; suggested minimum
CSR form 43; waste production
and disposal 65–6, 98; water
consumption 64–5
environmental initiatives 6; Global
Reporting Initiative (GRI) level A
reporting 20; ISO 26000 (2010) 17;
*OECD Guidelines for Multinational
Enterprises* 14; UN Global Compact,
Ten Principles **16**
Environmental Profit & Loss (EP&L) 103
equity analysts, opinion of CSR ratings
5–6
ESG: Environmental, Social and
corporate Governance: and fiduciary
duty 33; PUMA (PPR Home) study
application to 105
European Sustainable Investment
Forum (Eurosif) 2, 33
EuroSOX 82–3, 99n2
evidence 23–6, 50, 59–60, 66, 69, 78–80,
82–3, 88–94
extra-financial factors 33

fatalities *see* social data, fatalities
finance, *OECD Guidelines for
Multinational Enterprises* 14
financial boundaries within CSR
reporting 35
financial performance 4; CSR effect on
6, 10
Financial Times, integrated reporting
movement gaining momentum 46–7
food products, milk scandal 5
formulas: CO_{2e} equivalents 125; CSR
factor 127; energy 126; Full-Time
Equivalents (FTE) 126; Lost Time
Injuries (LTI) 126; pollution ratios
126; Price CO2 (P/CO2) 128; Price
CSR (P/CSR) 127; Price Pollution
(P/ Pollution) 127; Return on
Pollution (ROP) 127
FTSE All Share Index 4
fuel 18, 37, 61–6, 98–9, 104, 125–6
Fujitsu **13**
Full-Time Equivalents (FTE's) or
Headcounts *see* social data

gas *see* Greenhouse Gas (GHG) Protocol
gasoline 62, **86**, **132**
gender 56, 67, 70, 75, 80, 99n5
geographical office standards 50, 63–4,
80, 97–8
Global Reporting Initiative (GRI)
12–13, 18–22; criticisms of 20–2;
problems with content and quality
principles 58–60; sustainability rating
9; treatment of omissions 21
Global Warming Potential (GWP) 61
Goldman Sachs 10
governance, organizational, ISO 26000
(2010) 17
governance data: audit committee
meetings 76; board meetings held 75;
board size 75; duration of auditor's
service 76, **131**, **133**; duration of board
member service 75, **131**, **133**; Global
500 best performing companies
analysis 109; study of 50 largest
companies' reports indicators 56–7;
study of 50 largest companies' reports
indicators on independent directors
57; suggested minimum CSR form
43; women on the board 75

greenhouse gas emissions 17–18, 25, 32n12, 35, 40–1, 46, 61, 63–4, 87, 104, 109, 125

Greenhouse Gas (GHG) Protocol **12**, 13; consolidation method, scoping definition 41; converters used in measurements of air travel 63; converters used in measurements of fuel consumption 61–3; description 17–18; double counting in conglomerates 40; leasing, effect on reporting 37; problems with 18

Greenhouse Gas Protocol: *A Corporate Accounting and Reporting Standard* (2001) **12**, 13

Guthrie, Lois 76n4, 116

Hawken, Paul 9

hazardous waste *see* waste

headcount *see* social data

Hewitt, Gordon 3n3, 116

human rights: Global Reporting Initiative (GRI) level A reporting 20; ISO 26000 (2010) 17; UN Global Compact, Ten Principles **16**

human rights data omitted in study of 50 largest companies' reports 58

hydrofluorocarbons (HFCs) 61, 125

incineration *see* waste, combustion

inconsistencies 9–10

information, connectivity, International <IR> Framework 27

integrated reporting of financial and non-financial data 43; audit statement: intelligibility, relevance, reliability and comparability 48; auditors and reviewers work compared 48–9; cash flow model as basis for CSR report 102–3; harmonizing financial and non-financial data 49; King III recommendations 46

International <IR> Framework, guiding principles and content 27–9

International Accounting Standards Board (IASB) 1, **13**; role in suggested mandatory CSR reporting 53

International Federation of Accountants (IFAC) 23

International Financial Reporting Standards (IFRS) 21; consistency in financial context, not in CSR data 40; gaps in requirements for CSR reporting 46; joint operations 39; leasing an asset or buying services 38; parallel data in financial report and CSR report 43

International Forbes Fortune 2000 companies *117–20*; anti-corruption data omitted in study of 50 largest companies' reports 58; *see also* environmental data; governance data; social data

International Integrated Reporting Council (IIRC) **13**, 13, 43; avoidance of AA1000 49; cash flow model as basis for CSR report 102; global authority 27

International Organization for Standardization (ISO) **13**

investment advisors, *Principles for Responsible Investments* (PRI 2005) 29–30

investment banks, *Principles for Responsible Investments* (PRI 2005) 29–30

investors 34–5, 100–3, 105–10; analysis of ESG performance 55; CSR reporting benefits 2, 100; data, standard, accessible and quantified to be useful 109–10; implications of CSR reporting 111; P/CSR calculation as basis for decision 106; P/E versus P/CSR *107*; role in suggested mandatory CSR reporting 49

investors, individual 5

investors, institutional: analysis of ESG performance 10; attractiveness of social responsible corporations 4; CSR and share prices 6; *Principles for Responsible Investments* (PRI 2005) 29–30

invoices *see* documentation

ISA 320 47

ISA 500 as model for evidence 78

ISAE 3000 13, 23–7; adequate, suitable, reliable evidence 78; auditor requirements 26–7; audits, non-financial 24; data types, documentable and probable 79–81; levels of assurance 24; risk of the task 25; signs of weak evidence *24*
ISO 26000 (2010) **13**, 16

joint operations (JOs): reporting decisions in operational boundaries 39–40; share of reporting in financial boundaries 39–40
joint ventures (JV's) 39, 41
J.P. Morgan 5

Kamp-Roelands, Nancy 48
kerosene 62, **86, 132**
key performance indicator (KPI) 2, 28, 34, *45*
Kinder Lyderberg Domini Research & Analytics *see* KLD index
King Report on Corporate Governance (2009) 46
KLD index: best in class screening 8; effect of good rating 5–6; negative screening of companies 8; positive screening 8
Kyoto Agreement 61

labor relations: Global Reporting Initiative (GRI) level A reporting 20; ISO 26000 (2010) 17; *OECD Guidelines for Multinational Enterprises* 14; safety standards reporting 38; UN Global Compact, Ten Principles **16**; *see also* social data
leasing 36–8, 51n11
leave, paid and unpaid 22, 69, 71
legal entities 41–2, 63, 74, 95–7
Lost Time Injuries Frequency (LTIF) 71–2, 83

Margolis, Joshua D. 6
materiality: AA1000AS 25; International <IR> Framework 27; ISAE 3000 25
materiality, financial, definition of in ISA 320 47
materiality, non-financial: AA1000 47; ISAE 3000 and 47

measurement equipment 79–80
measurements 2, 7, 9–10, 25, 28, 35, 41, 54, 75–80, *84*, 100
measurements, greenhouse gas 17–18, 36–7, 50, 61–4
methane (CH$_4$) 61
Microsoft Excel, disadvantages 95
Microsoft's SharePoint libraries/lists 94
Mogensen, Birgitte 100
monitoring 26, 83–4, 88–90, 93–4

Night, Dave 51n25, 115n1, 116
nitrous oxide (N$_2$O) 61
non-profit organizations, ISO 26000 (2010) 16
norm consumption *see* consumption
Novo Nordisk 101; integrated reporting of financial and non-financial data 46

OECD Guidelines for Multinational Enterprises (OECD 1976) **12**, 14
OECD Guidelines for Multinational Enterprises (OECD 2011) **12**, 13
oil 62, **86, 118–20, 132**
O'Mallley, Charles 51n24, 116

Passant, François 33
pay slips *see* documentation
perfluorcarbons (PFCs) 61, 125
price earnings (P/E) 106, *107–8*, 128
Price Pollution (P/ Pollution) 107, 127
Principles for Investors in Inclusive Finance (PIIF 2011) **13**, 30
Principles for Responsible Investments (PRI 2005) **13**, 29–30
product liability, Global Reporting Initiative (GRI) level A reporting 20
production 34–41
profit & loss (P&L) 98
profitability of social responsibility corporations: arguments for 4–5; data inconclusive and biased 7, 9; implications of CSR reporting 111; inconclusive 10; P/CSR calculation as basis for decision 106
public relations tool 1
PUMA (PPR Home) 103–4, 106, 107, 110n11